THE ERNIES BOOK

Dr Meredith Burgmann, well-known political agitator and international busybody has had a colourful criminal career including 21 arrests. She was an academic for twenty years, President of the NSW Legislative Council for eight and is a cricket tragic for life.

Dr Burgmann has written seriously on women's issues, particularly on pay equity. Her previous book on the boofy blokes of the BLF was a bestseller.

Yvette Andrews is a film maker, musician, community activist, AFL coach, Reg Reagan impersonator and senior bureaucrat. She juggles her various careers as well as looking after her six-month-old son.

Although she has never written a book she is sure she has more than one in her and has for many years practised the under-appreciated art of letter writing.

Both authors share a passion for Aboriginal art and the Sydney Swans.

Meredith Burgmann **&** Yvette Andrews

THE ERNIES BOOK

1000
terrible things
Australian men have
said about women

ALLEN&UNWIN

First published in 2007

Copyright © Meredith Burgmann and Yvette Andrews 2007

Cover illustration, internal icons and chapter heading illustrations © Fiona Katauskas, 2007.

All other cartoons featured remain under the copyright of the original illustrators: Warren Brown, Rod Clement, Jenny Coopes, Rocco Fazarri, Lindsay Foyle, Bill Leak, Bruce Petty, Ron Tandberg, Cathy Wilcox.

Allen & Unwin
83 Alexander Street
Crows Nest NSW 2065
Australia
Phone: (61 2) 8425 0100
Fax: (61 2) 9906 2218
Email: info@allenandunwin.com
Web: www.allenandunwin.com

National Library of Australia
Cataloguing-in-Publication entry:

Burgmann, Meredith, 1947- .
      The Ernies book : 1000 terrible things Australian men have said about women.
      Includes index.

      ISBN 978 1 74175 392 9 (pbk.).

      1. Sex discrimination against women - Australia. 2. Sexism - Australia.
      3. Faux pas - Australia. I. Andrews, Yvette. II. Title.

 305.42

Set in 10.5/13.5 pt Warnock Pro by Kirby Stalgis
Cover design by Kirby Stalgis
Printed in Australia by McPherson's Printing Group

10 9 8 7 6 5 4 3 2 1

contents

awards key

Ernies award winners are indicated throughout the chapters by icons representing their category. For a complete list of winners see the Dishonour Board at the end of the book.

 The Gold Ernie

 The Silver Ernie for the industrial category

 The Silver Ernie for the judicial category

 The Silver Ernie for the media category

 The Silver Ernie for the political category

 The Warney for the sporting category

 The Fred for the clerical/culinary/celebrity category

 The Clinton for repeat offenders

 The Anon or Good Ernie

 The Elaine for remarks by women least helpful to the sisterood

introduction
booze and boos

It is very appropriate that this book on Australian male chauvinism comes out in the Year of the Golden Pig, an important Chinese anniversary that only comes round every 60 years. It is very propitious and signifies wealth for all concerned. We hope that means this book will be a bestseller.

The book charts the history of 15 years of the Ernie Awards for sexist remarks by Australian men. We started with well over a thousand quotes but, because of technical reasons and downright fear, have had to remove some particular shockers.

We think it is a rollicking good read but, more importantly, it is accurate and academically respectable. We have authenticated the name, title and year for each outrageous remark. We hope that Australians will not only buy this book for Christmas stockings, but that it becomes a serious tool for media and gender studies courses.

From humble beginings in 1993 as the mock celebration of the life's work of an infamous sexist the annual Ernie Awards soon grew to be Australia's premier celebration of oral sexism.

The ceremony was held in August or September each year, so the 'Ernies year' followed this timetable. Although a year might be described as 2003, it actually encompasses late 2002 up to August 2003. We collected quotes throughout the year, always believing that no one would say anything terrible and the event would be a total failure. But we were never disappointed!

There were a number of distinguishing features of the Awards ceremonies. The judging process was robust and democratic. Nominations were judged by the level of booing and jeering they received. Experienced Boo Monitors were appointed to determine the most derided remark in each category. This high pressure job was taken very seriously, and to ensure the wishes of the crowd were accurately reflected the Boo Monitors would often call for a boo-off.

Each woman who nominated a man who won their particular category was presented with one of the tasteful Silver Ernie trophies. The nominator of the ultimate winning quote of that year got the Gold Ernie trophy. Male winners occasionally asked if they could have the trophy and from time to time we agreed.

We always began with an Aboriginal Welcome to Country. This was usually performed by Judy Chester or Millie Ingram, who would plead for us to get the proceedings started so they could get on with having a good time. Each year we tried to celebrate a significiant anniversary for women and we would always hold a raffle to raise money for women involved in important struggles.

Despite the jaundiced views of our critics, anyone who wanted to come was invited. You got onto the Ernies invitation list by simply asking and you got into the Ernie Awards ceremony by wearing a nice frock. The strict dress code was either themed to one of the anniversaries we were celebrating, or just appealed to the spirit of the times. In latter years there was a fiercely competitive 'frock-off' which was judged by a celebrity style critic admist wild cheering and shameless showing off.

Another fascinating feature of the Ernie Awards was the enormous interest shown by the international press in this bizarre Australian event. Our favourite publication was the *Taipei Times.*

You will see that there was no party political bias in the nominations. There are deserving winners from all sides of politics. The serial offenders trophy, known as the Clinton, is probably the only time when vindictiveness and political one sidedness was shown.

We have included famous people saying inane things and occasionally nobodies saying extraordinary things or something that illustrated a particular genre of Australian sexism. Sometimes the comments are not so much sexist as silly. Sometimes nice people say things that they probably shouldn't have. Anything that was really funny always made the cut.

Otherwise unknown personalities have suddenly become famous because the Ernies highlighted their shocking remarks. They include style consultant Mark Patrick, Jeff Corbett from the *Newcastle Herald*, and lesser known politicians such as Martin Ferguson and Robert Oakeshott. Listen boys, we made you.

Although there is an Ernies maxim that you can't get an Ernie for trying, occasionally try-hards have slipped through the process and are pretty obvious.

For those men who claim we have taken them out of context, we probably have, but it's up to them to prove to us that they were actually saying something nice about women before we will apologise. To Paddy McGuinness and Piers Akerman, who are going to write mean columns about us, don't forget that all publicity is good publicity, and please spell our names correctly.

Throughout the years we have found a number of issues that quite obviously get up women's noses and these are represented in this collection.

The first is the issue of 'merit'. Merit has always been a male-judged quality, and the endless politicians that talk about there not being enough women of merit for particular positions have obviously read no academic work on the concept. The definition of merit is manipulated by whoever is trying to replicate themselves in positions of power.

The second issue which got women hot under the transverse lapels was that of ageism. This was best illustrated by the way in which an unknown style consultant from Sydney beat all comers for his comment that sleeveless dresses were a bad look on women over 30 years old.

Any suggestion that women's sport was not important upset the sports fans amongst us and the idea that professional women were ball-breaking dragons always caused offence. And finally, anything in the media describing disagreements between two women as a cat fight, or which had the word 'claws' in it, really gave the women the roaring s....!

We have had great fun trying to decide how to describe this book. We wanted there to be a sealed section on hooters and a fold out poster of Shane Warne. We thought the introduction should be written by Warney's mum, and believe the launch should consist of the placement of a Golden Pig in the pavement outside the Oxford Tavern (a Sydney pub famous for jelly wrestling and lingerie lunches). And finally, we want to knock *Spotless* off the bestseller list, trumpeting 'from women who hate stains to women who hate men'.

There are many people we need to thank for the 15 years of Ernies celebrations. First of all we want to thank all those journalists, presumably women, who tracked down these terrible things said by politicians, sportsmen or judges and reproduced them in the media. We also want to thank the gossip columnists who accurately report the lives of male celebrities.

We want to thank all the cartoonists for so beautifully nailing the inappropriateness of certain remarks, especially Cathy Wilcox and Jenny Coopes, who must wake up every morning as angry as we are. We also want to thank journalist Debra Jopson for her annual Ernies preview, which was always an excellent analysis of the field though it never managed to pick the winner.

We want to thank the women of the National Pay Equity Coalition who have been the serious sponsors of the Ernies from the beginning—Philippa Hall, Clare Burton, Di Fruin, Juliet Richter, Anita Devos, Fran Hayes, Suzanne Hammond, Suzanne Jamieson, Danny Blackman, Martina Nightingale, Meg Smith and those of the Civil Dead who because of their senior public service roles cannot be seen to be actively involved in fomenting discontent.

We especially want to thank Kerry Sanderson, one of the most serious people we know, who sat stunned through the early Ernies, appreciating the serious intent but not so sure about some of the light-hearted antics; octogenarian Margaret Jones, who would turn up each year with a bundle of tatty newpaper clippings harbouring a gold mine of terrible quotes; and Helen Randerson for her terrier-like investigative skills.

Thanks to everyone who helped organise the Ernies functions—Jo Tilly, Lesley Gruit, Zoe Backes, Helen Buttigieg, Rose Tracey, Jackie Trad, Claudine Lyons, Amanda Tattersall, Zoe Taylor, Sarah-Jane Collins, Jason Stewart, Damien Spruce, Oli McColl, Andrew Hanson, John Graham, Paul Tracey, Joel Conomos and Andrew Beattie—for putting up with the hysterical requests from Ernies women trying to change their dinner bookings at the last minute and complaining about the table arrangements. And of course we would like to thank the long suffering Parliament House catering staff.

We'd like to thank the photographers for capturing all the historic, the serious and the silly moments—Justine Muller, Rose Tracey, Owen Andrews, Moya Dodd, Fiona Katauskas and Sue Tracey.

And thank you to all the guest presenters, Boo Monitors and frock-off competitors over the years.

Finally to those who have asked if the Ernies will continue—if men keep making sexist remarks, then the Ernies will keep punishing them for it!

1993

In the beginning...

Just as no one remembers who Oscar actually was, few people remember the original Ernie. However, women in the trade union movement in the 1980s and 1990s recall him well.

Ernie Ecob was the secretary of the AWU, the old Shearers' Union, and was famous for his comment that women only wanted to be shearers for the sex.[1] He also failed to endear himself to women in many other ways. In fact as Charlie Oliver, the previous AMW secretary who appointed Ernie to the job said, 'I've made a blue. I've put a yobbo in as secretary.'

---

1   But that's what we thought the sheep were for.

Those of us involved in the trade union movement in New South Wales had battled with him on many occasions. So in May 1993 when he announced his resignation, Vicki Telfer from the Commonwealth Public Service Union suggested that we have a lunch to celebrate. And that's how it all began. We also realised that it was exactly 10 years since the 'Women in Unions Caucus' had been formed and decided to celebrate that occasion at the same time.

The Women in Unions Caucus was established after another famous case of industrial sexism. In 1983 Barrie Unsworth, Secretary of the NSW Labor Council, announced support for the Miss Australia Quest. When the women delegates began hissing and jeering, he snapped back at us, 'Miss Australia wouldn't face much competition from you lot if she came down here.' We of course stormed out. Eventually Barrie apologised and we all trooped back in. Many years later he said it was the most embarrassing moment of his political life.

But some of our supporters amongst the male unionists hadn't quite got the point. At the pub afterwards, one said, 'Never mind dear, I think you're pretty.' So basically the first Ernies function was started by women unionists to protest at sexism in the trade union movement. However, it grew from there.

The invitation to that first awards celebration announced a grand farewell dinner at NSW Parliament House for Ernie (Women don't belong in Shearing Sheds) Ecob and proclaimed that there would be a presentation of the Ernie Ecob Memorial Trophy for the most bestial remark of the year.

The trophy featured a miniature portrait of Ernie Ecob and a sheep rampant atop a brass plinth, a reference to Ernie's origins in the Shearers' Union. Guests were advised to wear a 'good frock—something Ernie would approve of' and 40 women came, suitably attired.

The winner of the inaugural Ernie Ecob Memorial Trophy was the National Secretary of the Shop Distributive and Allied Employees Association, Joe de Bruyn, for his remark: 'All childcare subsidies should be removed and reallocated to women who stayed home to mind their children.'

When the *Sydney Morning Herald* informed Ernie of this event, he retorted, 'It's the most ridiculous thing I've ever heard of . . . what do you expect, they've never liked me and I've never liked them.' And then of course went on to totally endorse the remarks of the inaugural winner: 'Joe has done the right thing . . . children should have the full care of their mother . . . I believe ninety per cent of the problems of this country have been caused by the breakdown of the family unit.'

In a propitious coincidence, as we enjoyed ourselves the Honourable Elaine Nile from the religiously conservative Call to Australia Party was making a speech a few metres away in the NSW Legislative Council. Elaine attacked our celebration of Ernie's retirement: 'The Call to Australia Group strongly supports the positive pro-family views expressed by Mr Joe de Bruyn . . . In spite of the vicious attack and ridicule directed at Mr Joe de Bruyn by the so-called loony left, the left wing women's caucus, and the sarcastic presentation of the so-called Ernie Ecob Award for the most sexist remark of the year, we believe the majority of women support Mr de Bruyn.'

We all had a wonderful time and promised to repeat the exercise the next year.

1994

keep them nervous!

The second annual Ernie Awards celebrated the 25th anniversary of the 1969 equal pay decision. Because of the blow out in nominations, four categories of Silver Ernies were devised (Judicial, Political, Media and Industrial). These were recognised by the awarding of trophies featuring a very tasteful piglet on a multicoloured plinth.

We also offered an award for those who had attempted to clean up their act. It was named the 'Gareth' after the time Gareth Evans offered to jump across the table and garrotte Bronwyn Bishop. (Later, this award had to have its name changed.)

Another new category which proved to be a great hit with the Ernies women, as personal bile and bigotry rose to the fore, was for women whose remarks were least helpful to the sisterhood. We named it after the Honourable Elaine Nile, who had so cruelly attacked us the previous year. Elaine was always very sanguine about the naming of this award and would ask after a successful Ernies night who had won her award and was it possible for her to have it.

Because of the difficulty of finding appropriate trophies, the Elaine trophy was a female body-builder in a bikini and the Gareth was a debating trophy of a man speaking, of course.

As this occasion was so obviously based on the Logie Awards, we assumed the winner would be chosen beforehand and revealed from an elegant envelope by a guest presenter. However, the women of the Ernies functions have a mind of their own. TV presenter Stan Grant was selected prior to the ceremony as the winner of the Media Silver Ernie for his enthusiastic endorsement of an anti-cellulite créme which later turned out not to work. This was a big mistake.

In a display that later became known as the 'boo-off', the crowd vehemently rallied behind Peter Smark and Bernard Zuel for their series in the *Sydney Morning Herald*, 'Why Professional Women Can't Get a Man'. Under the weight of women power they were eventually declared the winner. This began the tradition of awarding Ernies based on the level of boos and jeers that remarks engendered, as judged by highly trained Boo Monitors.[1]

The year 1994 was also significant because of the outrage caused by comments made by judicial figures. This was to be a feature of the early Ernies years but, after much media coverage and, we believe, relentless attention from the Ernies, judges became less sexist or at least more discreet.

And for the first time the saying which was to become the Ernies war cry was picked up in the media—'Keep them nervous!'

---

1   Women selected from the crowd based on their commitment to having a good time.

JUDGE JOHN EWEN BLAND, VICTORIAN COUNTY COURT
Commenting on a rape trial:
It does happen in the common experience of those who have been in the law as long as I have that 'no' often subsequently means 'yes.'

PETER SMARK AND BERNARD ZUEL,
SYDNEY MORNING HERALD
Wrote a newspaper series called:
Why Professional Women Can't Get a Man

TERRY GRIFFITHS, NSW LIBERAL MINISTER
In response to allegations of sexually harassing his staff:
I honestly believe that my personal behaviour was in a family mode. They're like my own kids. I'm a toucher . . . I have a habit of touching people in that regard. I'm old fashioned.

JOHN DAWKINS, FEDERAL TREASURER
To Liberal MP, Kathy Sullivan:
Sweetheart, you don't need a model to work this one out.

STAN GRANT, TV PRESENTER
Enthusiastically endorsed a miracle anti-cellulite thigh crème.
Six months later he told us it didn't work!

LANCE JAMIESON, UNION OFFICIAL
Creatively used his union-provided credit card at the
Sydney brothel A Touch of Class.

ROBERT WEBSTER, NSW NATIONAL PARTY MINISTER
Responding to a question about women employees:
This must be ladies' day in the Legislative Council.

JOE THOMPSON,
FORMER VEHICLES BUILDERS UNION OFFICIAL
In his newspaper article 'Academic Feminists Hurting Families':
*The trendy new expression, 'Quality Child Care', can never take the place of
a mother caring and loving her children in a home and family environment.*

JUSTICE DEREK BOLLEN,
SOUTH AUSTRALIAN SUPREME COURT

There is, of course, nothing wrong with a husband, faced with his wife's initial refusal to engage in intercourse, in attempting, in an acceptable way, to persuade her to change her mind and that may involve rougher than usual handling.

PETER NAGLE, NSW LABOR MP

Said male perpetrators of domestic violence were 'just decent citizens'.

1995

i do

The year 1995 was an overflow affair with some of the women having to eat in the kitchen. The dress code was 'nice frock', although the invitation stipulated that the style police would allow 'anything but dark-coloured stockings with pale slingbacks'. It was announced that 'the judges' decisions were final and disputations would occur over lunch'.

The invitation also acknowledged that we were celebrating the 20th anniversary of International Women's Day, and the proceeds of the raffle would go to the women involved in the Hindmarsh Bridge case. This became the one serious part of the Ernie Awards—the large amounts of money we raised through the raffle each year always went to women's organisations involved in important struggles.

For the first time there was some indication that male chauvinists around Australia were in fact becoming deeply anxious. The annual ritual of men ringing up to find out what they had been nominated for began. Some nominees even asked if it was at all possible to have their name removed from the short list.

Another important Ernie maxim was created at the 1995 awards ceremony, when Sydney shock jock Ron Casey was nominated and we ruled him out on the grounds that 'you can't get an Ernie for trying'.

Guest presenter Ann Sherry awarded the Elaine to Blanche d'Alpuget for simply saying, 'I do'.

It also became clear that being named Ernie was now a problem. Poor Ernie Page, the NSW Labor frontbencher, had already started being teased because of his name. He was in fact later to win two Gareths for men behaving better!

According to one media report the popularity of the lunch showed it filled 'a gaping hole for women to get pissed and make fun of men'. And Ken Dickin from radio station 5AAA inadvertently ended up being nominated for saying, during an interview about the ceremony, 'Oh, the girls will be as full as googs by then.'

JEFF WELLS, FAIRFAX SPORTS WRITER

Do we want Cathy Freemans who look like Mal Meningas or Melinda Gainsfords who look like Hulk Hogan? Meanwhile, I would like to see Cathy in a new event in 2000. Call it the 400 metres for women who still look like women.

ALEXANDER DOWNER,
LEADER OF THE FEDERAL OPPOSITION

Joked about calling the Liberal Party's domestic violence policy: *The Things that Batter.*

SENATOR NOEL CRICHTON-BROWNE,
WESTERN AUSTRALIAN LIBERAL MP

Threatened a woman journalist if she reported how he voted.
I will screw your tits off.

She explained her job was to report the news so NCB said:
Would you like to have sex with me tonight? Write that down.

MICHAEL HODGMAN, TASMANIAN LIBERAL MP

*Extreme lesbian elements which have infiltrated the ALP are delighted
with their success; the merit principle has been thrown out the window;
and, Keating has weakly capitulated to the man-haters . . .
The Mad As A March Hare radical feminists have got the Labor Party
firmly by the testicles—and they will not let go.*

MARTIN FERGUSON, ACTU PRESIDENT

Called women unionists campaigning for paid maternity leave:
hairy legged femocrats

P.P. MCGUINNESS, FAIRFAX COLUMNIST

On sexual harassment:

*What male has not occasionally been subject to the unwanted
attentions of a female, even in trivial matters such as picking
imaginary threads from a jacket lapel.*

PORT STEPHENS TIMES

The typical feminists are the sort of people who interpret a harmless peck on the cheek or a quick pinch on the bum as being sexual harassment.

JUSTICE JEFFERY SPENDER,
QUEENSLAND FEDERAL INDUSTRIAL COURT

It's not unknown for a woman to sleep her way to the top.

MICHAEL LAVARCH, FEDERAL ATTORNEY-GENERAL

The judge [Jeffery Spender] said nothing which should be taken as in any way demeaning or stereotyping of women.

MURRAY TOBIAS, QC,
PRESIDENT OF THE BAR ASSOCIATION

Sleeping her way to the top is perhaps a crude way of putting it, but it's a fact of life. I don't see why women should take offence at a judge stating the blatantly obvious.

ALBY SHULTZ, NSW LIBERAL MP

Clover Moore MP is a disgrace to her gender and she is for what all decent women are against. She's all for breaking down traditional values and cutting away the democractic rights of the timber industry.

P.P. MCGUINNESS, FAIRFAX COLUMNIST

There are two groups of middle-aged feminists—those who are still striving for an advancement for which few of them are qualified (the 'sisters in suits') and those who are total failures and blame it all on men.

JIM O'MAHONY, TOOHEYS MANAGING DIRECTOR

When employees took industrial action before Christmas
he cancelled the work Christmas party saying:

Put it this way, if you find your new wife in bed with another man, she still can't expect you to take her out to the wedding celebrations.

PIERS AKERMAN, NEWS LIMITED COLUMNIST

On the United Nations Fourth World Women's Conference:

SISTERS OF INDULGENCE: 40,000 middle class women will brandish their fringe ideology at yet another junket.

PETER RUEHL, OPINION WRITER

I don't mean to put down this women's conference, it's just that I can't even remember where they held the last one. If Beijing is anything to go on, it was probably in Sarajevo.

PIERS AKERMAN, NEWS LIMITED COLUMNIST

The politics of feminism do not rest well with journalism, probably because to subscribe to the worship of the current crop of feminist super heroines requires a suspension of disbelief.

AUSTRALIAN WORKERS UNION (ERNIE'S UNION)

As part of a campaign to attract new members, this male dominated union offered discount strippers from Frisky Business.

JOHN SEBERRY, WOLLONGONG MAGISTRATE

I'll never understand the stupidity . . . of women who get beaten up and then, contrary to [domestic violence] orders, go back to live with the [offender]. They must like that sort of treatment.

JUSTICES CROCKETT AND TEAGUE, VICTORIAN SUPREME COURT

Reduced the sentence of a man who had admitted raping and imprisoning a woman because it was not:

a very grave case of rape.

MICHAEL LEUNIG, CARTOONIST FOR *THE AGE*

Thoughts of baby lying in a childcare centre—This famous cartoon began 'I can't believe it! My own mother who I want to be with more than anything in the world . . . dumps me here in this horrendous crèche . . .'. Leunig exercised his right to deny us permission to reproduce his cartoon referring to us as 'narrow puritan hoons who tag along with gender politics'.

MIKE GIBSON, MEDIA IDENTITY

Today I want to devote this column to Kate Fischer, firstly because she's got big boobs and secondly because she seems to be the only woman left in this country capable of telling the truth.

BRIAN WILSHIRE, TALK-BACK RADIO HOST

If you were a martian observing Earth and looked at magazines and publications produced for half of the population, who would you choose to govern the country? The ones interested in flower arrangements and macrame, or the ones interested in mechanical things?

JEFF WELLS, FAIRFAX SPORTS WRITER

On women tennis players receiving the same prize money as men: *Yesterday at Flinders Park another chapter was written in the book of weird excesses in the fight for equality.*

STAN ZEMANEK, TALK-BACK RADIO HOST

Stan: Some women do provoke men into belting them.

Caller: Do you think so?

Stan: I'm sure of it.

Caller: Gee.

Stan: I'm sure of it. There are some women out there who just can't help themselves, who nag, nag, nag, scream, scream, scream, and somewhere along the line someone's got to break.

JUDGE LES DOWNS, NSW DISTRICT COURT

His Honour: You said Miss –

Hughes: Hughes, Ms Hughes.

His Honour: Mrs or Miss?

Hughes: Ms. M-s.

His Honour: I don't understand that. Are you Mrs or Miss?

Hughes: Ms, your Honour, M-s.

His Honour: Yes. Yes, Ms Hughes...

1996

it's not like it's the maltese falcon

The 1996 Ernies was so overcrowded hundreds of women had to be knocked back. Some women were instructed not to eat, but at least they would 'look good in their nice frocks'. The boo-offs came into their own and many categories were hotly contested.

This year we celebrated the 30th anniversary of the abolition of the Federal Government's bar on employment for married women and women at last took seriously the idea that they were part of the nomination process. The Teachers Federation women sent in a number of rippers, which proved that they had spent many women hours poring over the daily papers.

There was only one nomination in the Industrial category and that was for the Labor Council of NSW, but no one could think of a specific quote. Did this mean the end of trade union sexism? Maybe not—the lucky door prize was the Labor Council tape of its 110th anniversary function where there were nine male speakers and no women.

Peter Costello's nomination in the political category for saying 'If you don't like my tie, blame my mother' began the important Ernie tradition of men blaming their mums.

Engagement from the media had moved from treating us as a quaint curio to all out attack. The *Telegraph Mirror's* Piers Akerman, surprise, surprise, wrote, 'Only those with current trade union cards need forward their material and appropriately the judges include such irrelevant extremists as Meredith Burgmann MLC, the Left Wing dinosaur of the NSW Upper House and Dr

Dale Spender the feminist author.' Other media try-hards, Ron Casey and P.P. McGuinness, were ruled out of contention because once again we had to stress that you can't get an Ernie for trying.

Journalist Jeff Wells, whose main claim to fame is winning Ernie Awards, made some particularly harsh comments about the *Telegraph Mirror* photograph of Yvette Andrews and Ann Summers at the ceremony. 'Yvette is the one on the left looking suitably rubicund in a nifty burlap Muu Muu by Kristoff of Kogarah[1] Ann is the blonde on the right in the "Guys and Dolls" powersuit by Harry of Hurstville.' Once again, Jeff, you can't get an Ernie for trying.

He went on, 'It is typical of the cheapskates of the women's movement that they refuse to give me my hard earned silver Ernie trophy which I won last week . . . I mean it's not like it's the Maltese Falcon.'

---

1   It was a fabulous red frock (author)

PAT CALDWELL, BYRON BAY MAGISTRATE

To a female defendant:

Come back when your IQ is as high as your skirt.

BOB MANSFIELD, JOHN FAIRFAX CEO

Don't expect that you can jump a step on the corporate ladder simply because you are women.

PIERS AKERMAN, NEWS LIMITED COLUMNIST

For 30 years the Australian feminist movement has been dominated by the women-who-want-to-be-men brigade.

PETER RUEHL, OPINION WRITER

If Carmen [Lawrence] is feminism's last hope, they sure got to the bottom of the barrel pretty quickly.

PETER COSTELLO, FEDERAL TREASURER

If you don't like my tie, blame my mother.

BOB CARR, NSW PREMIER

To Australian journalist Deborah Hope:

Your career high point was collecting Annita Keating's dry cleaning.

PETER WEST, ACADEMIC WRITER

When radical feminists rattle their sabres, the Labor Party rattles its knees.

RON GETHING, PERTH MAGISTRATE

Found a man not guilty of stalking a woman for seven years:
I don't think he was intimidating her, he was just being persistent.
He was being like a little puppy dog wagging its tail.

CRAIG GOLDINGS,
SYDNEY MORNING HERALD PHOTOGRAPHER

Shot of a man's face and women's bodies

KEN CALLANDER, RACING COMMENTATOR

Being of the old school, I won't concede women are better than men at very much.

MICHAEL BIDDULPH,
CHAIR OF THE EQUAL OPPORTUNITY TRIBUNAL

In a sexual harassment case he questioned why a woman had
not been asked for sexual favours:

Why would that be? I mean, she is not unattractive.

P.P. MCGUINNESS, FAIRFAX COLUMNIST

*The Biddulph comment is, as usual, being used as yet another springboard
for the ongoing campaign by official feminists to gain ideological control
over the judiciary and quasi-judiciary.*

KEN FARROW,
CEO OF THE AUSTRALIAN FINANCIAL MARKETS ASSOCIATION

*The dealing room [of the Stock Exchange] is male dominated,
with a style and function not suited to the female personality.*

PIERS AKERMAN, NEWS LIMITED COLUMNIST

Feminists have played a disastrous part in social policy over the past decade.

JEFF WELLS, FAIRFAX SPORTS WRITER

On the campaign by women tennis players for equal prize money:
WOMEN'S BOYCOTT TOO GOOD TO BE TRUE:
Now that this thing is up and running, let's strive to keep
women's tennis at the Open down to the bare minimum.

ROBERT OAKESHOTT, NSW NATIONAL PARTY CANDIDATE

My girlfriend is studying in Queensland and when she has
her degree and has learnt to cook, then I'll marry her.

REV. FRED NILE, NSW CHRISTIAN DEMOCRAT MP

Advocated a breath-testing regime in Parliament because:
Some women MPs become 'giggly' after a couple of glasses too many.

BOB CARR, NSW PREMIER

On Liberal MP Kerry Chikarovski's deep voice:
She must be on hormone treatment.

JOHN HOWARD, PRIME MINISTER

Issued an edict that women were not allowed to wear pants in his office.

BOB KATTER, FEDERAL NATIONAL PARTY MP

He [Mr Burgess] is also making the Leichhardt seat a testing ground for those who are game to defy the politically correct enviro-nazis and femo-nazis and all the rest of those little slanty-eyed ideologues who persecute ordinary average Australians.

RON GENTLE, NSW MAGISTRATE

Refused a request from the defendant's lawyer for a male witness to be directed to refer to the defendant as 'Ms X' rather than:

that piece over there.

1997

a lot of fussy old chooks

The year 1997 was the first time we held the awards ceremony as a dinner. Although we now had space for 400, we still had problems fitting everyone in.

We celebrated the 20th anniversary of the Anti-Discrimination Act. The invitation declared that 'the judges' decision is obviously not final as much disputation occurs' and this was certainly the case this time. It was also the year that heralded the first of the 'frock-offs'. A high standard was set, with Justice Lee Drake taking out the poshest frock award.

There were a record 80 nominations and once again those nominated displayed some anxiety. Nick Whitlam wrote to us, 'I see from today's *SMH* that I am a candidate for an Ernie tonight. Although I realise it will not disqualify me and will only marginally diminish the likelihood of me receiving an award, you should know that the correct quote is . . .'

We went truly national with Joan Kirner and Julia Gillard from Victoria nominating Jeff Kennett for his particularly offensive quote about Grammar girls.

We also made Ernies history with the nomination of an entire family— David Barnett, Pru Goward and Kate Fischer were all nominated. Pru Goward responded by calling us 'a lot of fussy old chooks' and accused us of 'rubbing our little Mao suits and wanting to go back to the Cultural Revolution'.

The Gold Ernie win by Olympics Minister Michael Knight made it clear that any statement which implies that the reason women don't get positions is because they're decided on 'merit, not sex' is particularly galling to women.

It was a jolly night enjoyed by many newcomers, including an entire table from Beecroft Rotary Club, with one of the prizes in the raffle being preselection for the safe ALP seat of Sydney.

JAMIE FAULKNER,
SYDNEY MORNING HERALD 'METRO' LIFTOUT

With women, as with fish, you have to know which sparkly insect to stick on the end of your thing to reel in the big ones.

JEFF WELLS, FAIRFAX SPORTS WRITER

But many sports fans believe that females appeal more when they are perceived as women— not as muscle-bound second-rate males. Compare today's lot to the slim, feminine, smooth muscle sprinters who used to win Olympic medals.

JOHN LAWS, BROADCASTER

It is the truth, isn't it, most chairpersons are men? . . . The best argument for bringing back the word chairman is just good old-fashioned honesty.

JACK THOMPSON, AUSTRALIAN FILM LEGEND

When launching the Sydney Olympic mascots:
Sure, the echidna is prickly but then that is modelled on the true Australian woman—you have to handle them very carefully.

MICHAEL KNIGHT, MINISTER FOR THE OLYMPICS

On why there were no women on the SOCOG Board:
Appointments are made on merit, not sex.

GERALD STONE, MEDIA IDENTITY

For a start, think of the thousands of families who have broken up under pressure to conform to New Age theories about sexual 'equality' and children's 'liberation'. Who'll make amends to them?

HUTTON GIBSON, MEL'S FATHER

Female priests: *untraditional*
Contraception: *a perversion*

DAVID BARNETT,
AUTHOR AND HUSBAND OF PRU GOWARD, THE PRIME
MINISTER'S ADVISER ON WOMEN'S ISSUES

Women would be happy to stay at home and look after the kids:
once we're through the present period.

COURIER MAIL

*Olympic women's hockey would not attract a
big crowd even if the teams played nude.*

TERRY SMYTH, FAIRFAX COLUMNIST

*Meanwhile, the NSW Government will kick off an inquiry into the value of
women's work including, for the first time, an estimate of the value of 'emotional
labour' as opposed to 'manual and intellectual labour'. You have to wonder
what could be next. The dollar value of a bad-hair day?*

JEFF WELLS, FAIRFAX SPORTS WRITER

*Mary Pierce, was in shocking shape as she sank like a stone in the
second round. Even her pout was overweight . . . When I reported this,
the feminasties from the Women in Sport and Blundstone
Workboots Unit howled.*

MIKE GIBSON, MEDIA IDENTITY

Most men, from my experience, prefer to keep the reason for their marriage breakdown to themselves. Many women, on the other hand, are so bitter that they feel they must shout it to the world.

DAVID NASON, NEWS LIMITED JOURNALIST

Described Helen Bauer, the new head of the NSW Department of Community Services, as:

Prim and schoolmarmish with a neat and grey world view, like a guard from the old television soap, Prisoner.

MICHAEL DUFFY, PUBLISHER

These days Australian novels are unadventurous and frequently similar to each other. Most of them are produced by and for women and consist of little more than emotional embroidery.

PETER MCKAY, FAIRFAX JOURNALIST

It's comforting to know sex is still used to sell cars. A survey by British magazine Maxim *rates French car-maker Peugeot as having the sexiest women in its advertisements . . . Okay let's lobby Peugeot and VW to have these ads shown here.*

JOHN FAIRFAX PHOTO SELECTOR

Chose this photo of Marie-Jose Perec's bottom to illustrate
her Atlanta Olympics 400 metres victory.

ARTHUR TUNSTALL, OLYMPIC OFFICIAL

*But [beach volleyball] is a good thing for television. You know, you see two girls in
nice little bikini costumes flopping themselves around and that's good for television.*

MARK PATRICK, ADVERTISING AGENT

*You have got this bunch of basically frustrated women who have decided
that if somebody is nude and she is on a poster, well it's offensive.*

JIM RUSSELL, CARTOONIST
Based 50 years of his cartoon strip, *The Potts,* on the same
old mother-in-law and dumb-wife joke.

PETER STERLING, RUGBY LEAGUE LEGEND
*Well I guess if you looked like this [photo of Paula Yates] you'd want to do
something . . . anything probably, because she didn't have anything
going for her before the surgery, now she's still a horror . . . but at least
she's a horror with bigger tits.*

MIKE GIBSON, MEDIA COMMENTATOR
*These Labor women amuse me . . . I mean one of their heroes is Joan Kirner.
Dear old Joan has done for Australian women's fashion what she did
to the economy of Victoria.*

BOB ELLIS, SPEECHWRITER AND AUTHOR
*The no fault divorce law has made marriage too easy-come easy-go, with
disastrous results for children . . . Many watch their mother go successively
to the bedroom with five or six male callers.*

MICHAEL WOOLDRIDGE, FEDERAL HEALTH MINISTER
*Medicare benefits may be withdrawn for lesbians seeking access to donor sperm
. . . I don't believe you can look at these things in a moral vacuum.*

TIM FISCHER, DEPUTY PRIME MINISTER

Fertility clinics will be over-run by aggressive lesbians at the expense of normal people.

IAN MCCULLOCH,
GRAND SECRETARY OF THE UNITED GRAND LODGE OF NSW

The minute you admit a woman member you change Freemasonry forever.

ROBERT RAY, LABOR SENATOR

Told Senator Amanda Vanstone she was so large she could:
double as a sight screen.

JOHN JUSTICE, PRESIDENT OF THE CAMPBELLTOWN
BRANCH OF THE YOUNG LIBERALS

*Men should be trained for war, women for the recreation of the warrior.
All else is folly.*

GREG SMITH, QC, PRESIDENT OF NSW RIGHT TO LIFE

*If women are able to buy abortion pills over the counter, that will mean there
will be too many hormones in their system without control.*

JUSTICE ALEC SOUTHWELL,
VICTORIAN SUPREME COURT

*A mature worldly woman is less likely to be traumatised
by a rape than an eighteen-year-old virgin.*

JEFF KENNETT, PREMIER OF VICTORIA

Referring to Opposition MPs John Brumby and John Thwaites:
Listen to the two girls from Melbourne Grammar on the other side.

RODERICK WEST,
CHAIR OF THE HIGHER EDUCATION REVIEW PANEL
Never run after a girl, a bus or an educational idea, because there
will be another one along in the next twenty minutes.

NOEL CRICHTON-BROWNE, LIBERAL SENATOR
To a female journalist:
I never realised before how ugly you are.

MAL COLSTON, INDEPENDENT SENATOR
Blamed his female office manager for his travel rorts:
I wish to make it perfectly clear at the outset that these overpayments
were caused by an inadequate bookkeeping system which was
in place at the time in my electorate office.

BRUCE RUXTON, RETURNED SERVICES LEAGUE
The government of Bob Carr is a disgrace . . . it even ruled that there is no
difference between a man who dresses as a woman and the genuine article.
Is that so? Tell that to a digger back from the front . . . A man is a man and
a woman is a woman. A man who dresses as a woman defies description
and I am in tune with Queen Victoria, who threw out a bill which was trying
to outlaw sexual relations between women. She could not for the life of her
imagine what they would do—neither can I. Keep up the good work, Piers.

JOHN HOWARD, PRIME MINISTER

Insisted that the term 'chairperson' not be used in 'any papers that come across the PM's desk'.

DAVID THOMAS,
FORMER ADVISER TO PAULINE HANSON

On women in politics:

PMT will be a valid reason for not attending council meetings or for kicking developers in the teeth. The second council meeting of the month will now take the form of a Tupperware party.

NICK WHITLAM, NRMA DIRECTOR

Notwithstanding her good looks, she is a mature woman, experienced in business and community affairs.

MARTIN FERGUSON,
SHADOW MINISTER FOR EMPLOYMENT AND TRAINING

To Democrat Leader Senator Cheryl Kernot, who happened to be sitting in the Hansard reporter's seat:

I always thought that was a woman's job. And you'll never get equal pay.

JOHN DE VRIES, HOOTERS RESTAURANT OWNER

The clothes our waitresses wear is nothing risqué.
When people go to the gym they wear less clothes.

JUDGE NIGEL CLARKE,
WESTERN AUSTRALIAN DISTRICT COURT

On the sexual abuse of children:
It is not necessarily going to be harmful in itself.

MIKE CARLTON, MEDIA IDENTITY

One of those great mysteries of life, such as, why can women only
read street directories when heading north.

DAVID HOOKES, FORMER AUSTRALIAN CRICKETER

I am actually dirty they caught him. The fact that he spent $13,000 in two days is
nothing to what my wife Robyn will do with the card. She has a black belt in shopping.
She shops off scratch. The card would have been safer with the bloke that stole it.

1998

wayward waiters and worthy winners

This year we celebrated the 10th anniversary of the founding of the National Pay Equity Coalition, the official host of the Ernies functions. The event was again packed. We even read out grovelling excuses from women who had not replied in time but still wanted a spot. We accepted 'being too depressed because of the Swans' slump in form' as a legitimate excuse.

That night, we consumed 229 bottles of house white, 78 house reds, 63 champagnes and numerous beers. The style police allowed anything, except for some reason yellow jumpers or platform sneakers. The quote for the night was from British feminist Edna O'Brien who said, 'The vote means nothing to women. We should be armed.'

A new award for repeat offenders was added. It was called the 'Clinton' for obvious reasons, and the nominees were John Laws, Paddy McGuinness, Piers Akerman, Pru Goward, Bettina Arndt and John Howard. John Howard won for failing to appoint a Sex Discrimination Commissioner for twelve months and refusing to recognise the term 'chairperson'. In bad taste, and because of the limited choice of appropriate trophies, the Clinton featured a man playing pool with some blue fabric stuck to the end of his cue.

One of the raffle prizes was a Spice Girls poster which showed we were still totally 'incorrect'. And the frock-off was won by a woman in a rather lovely Mao dress, a homage to Pru Goward's comments from the previous year.

One of the waiters introduced himself to us as Pauline Hanson's boyfriend and behaved in a most disgustingly sexist manner. He was, of course, comic

Godfrey Bigot. Some women didn't get the joke and kept complaining about the drunk waiter with his shirt sticking out his fly. Pauline Hanson herself did well with her continued attacks on single mothers. Perhaps that explains the ban on yellow jumpers.

An excellent quote from Boris Yelzin—'We must have a healthy space program in Russia; we need a return to the days when all little boys want to be cosmonauts, and all little girls want to be married to cosmonauts'—was ruled out because it was not Australian.

Lobbying began in earnest in 1998. Conversations were overheard in the ladies' room and out on the smoking balcony—'Well, we'll vote for Bettina in the Elaines if you support Piers in the other.' The voting (or rather booing) was particularly heated. The crowd was warned that dissent from the judges' decision was to be resolved by a boo-off and not in the car park afterwards.

Ernie Page won the Gareth for sacking sexist Maitland Council. He said he had 'greater motivation' because he wanted to show that 'even Ernies can be SNAGs'.

More importantly for many women, the Ernies were having a positive impact. The industrial newsletter, *Workforce*, reported 'HPM gets Ernie Raspberry. The AMWU hasn't had many wins in its long running equal remuneration battle with HPM. But it was successful this week in nominating the company for an Ernie award for . . . answering allegations of discrimination against women by sacking male comparators.'

JOHN LAWS, MEDIA IDENTITY

The greatest invention of any man is the purity of women.

PIERS AKERMAN, NEWS LIMITED COLUMNIST

Well, burn my bra. The old maids of the 1960s feminism are getting upset because the revolution has passed them by . . . That's right, the inconoclastic feminists of the 60s are lining up to get their heads read now as they ponder exactly where they went wrong and why their daughters don't write home any more.

DON TALBOT, AUSTRALIAN SWIMMING COACH
On swimmer Sam Riley:

There does come a time when you hang up your swimsuit because you become a wife or whatever.

BUSTER MOTTRAM, FAIRFAX SPORTS WRITER
On women's tennis:

The sisterhood has finally realised that it has been damaged commercially by a lack of femininity and, by association, with lesbianism. For example, no cosmetics companies (natural sponsors) are associated with women's tennis.

ROBERT MANNE, ACADEMIC

If the ALP is to prosper it must, in my opinion, emancipate itself from the stranglehold of a feminism which has lost touch with the diverse needs of women and families in the contemporary age.

PETER ROBINSON, FAIRFAX JOURNALIST

Pauline Hanson may be a dill, but she is a more successful feminist than almost anyone you can name.

TONY SMITH, QUEENSLAND LIBERAL MP
Women have a duty not to provoke men.

RUPERT MURDOCH, MEDIA MAGNATE
Favoured Lachlan instead of his oldest child Elizabeth
to take over News Limited:
*She has some things to work out. She has to decide how many kids
she is going to have and where she wants to live.*

JUDGE NIGEL CLARKE,
WESTERN AUSTRALIAN DISTRICT COURT
Gave a two year suspended sentence to a man for sexually
abusing his twelve-year-old stepdaughter:
*Indulgence is a pleasurable, curiosity-satisfying activity
by an intelligent precocious girl.*

BUSTER MOTTRAM, FAIRFAX SPORTS WRITER
Said paying women tennis players the same prize money as men was:
*a total capitulation to political correctness, following the constant harping
over a quarter century by vocal and belligerent American feminists.*

P.P. MCGUINNESS, FAIRFAX COLUMNIST

WHY EQUALITY WON'T WORK: The 50–50 rule must ultimately imply more incompetent women at the top than incompetent men . . .

IAIN MACLEAN, WESTERN AUSTRALIAN LIBERAL MP

They think they are the centre of the universe and will abort a baby just because it is inconvenient or summer is approaching and they want to wear a bikini.

P.P. MCGUINNESS, FAIRFAX COLUMNIST

. . . young women, tired of being preached at by raddled old feminists . . .

THE ANTARCTIC DIVISION OF THE FEDERAL ENVIRONMENT DEPARTMENT

Identified Weddell Hut at Mawson Station for heritage conservation
because its ceiling was covered with 92 pin-ups:
Weddell Hut is significant to Australia's cultural heritage.
This building is viewed affectionately by a number of
expeditioners and is renowned for its pin-ups.

THE *FINANCIAL REVIEW*

Accompanied a graph of the rising Australian dollar with a gratuitous
photo of Elle McPherson in a singlet with the caption:
Looking good, but will it last.

JAMIE FAULKNER,
SYDNEY MORNING HERALD 'METRO' LIFTOUT

As most female mammals die when they are no longer fertile, human
females seem to be outliving their usefulness by 30 or 40 years . . .

PAUL KELLY, MEDIA COMMENTATOR

At the Constitutional Convention:

You've got a wonderful array of women who add colour to the Chamber.

PETER WALSH, FORMER LABOR FEDERAL MP

On a speech by a delegate at the Constitutional Convention:

A rant from the unemployed social engineer Moyra Reyner about the necessity to protect in the preamble the rights of every identifiable group other than adult Anglo Celtic men.

ALAN JONES, TALK-BACK RADIO HOST

[Moira Reyner] is the woman with the colours in her hair. She's got the streaks in her hair, the pink bit at the front. She used to be an adviser to Joan Kirner when Joan was socially engineering Victoria into bankruptcy.

AN AUSTRALIAN SAILOR

In evidence to an Australian Defence Force Review:

Until then you will continue to have an outfit run by females and faggots. God help us if we ever go to war!

BILL LEAK, CARTOONIST FOR *THE AUSTRALIAN*
On the defection of Australian Democrats Leader
Cheryl Kernot to the Labor Party:

DON RANDALL, FEDERAL LIBERAL MP
Cheryl Kernot has the morals of an alley cat on heat.

DAILY TELEGRAPH
CHERYL GOES INTO LABOUR

THE *FINANCIAL REVIEW*
WUNDERFRAU TO WHORE

DAILY TELEGRAPH
BLONDE AMBITION

THE AUSTRALIAN
MADONNA-WHORE

CONWAY STENESNESS, CEO OF REVAMP
Wrote in the company newsletter:
*Michelle Coxeter from Australia Fair is up the duff and has a bun in the oven
. . . now she has a good use for those big bosoms of hers.*

JOHN HOWARD, PRIME MINISTER
Refused to guarantee the future of the Sex Discrimination Commissioner.

TIM FISCHER, DEPUTY PRIME MINISTER
The GST will greatly affect the workers of Australia . . . (pause) . . . and their wives.

PETER COSTELLO, FEDERAL TREASURER

Appeared at a press conference with the Minister for Women, Judi Moylan,
to talk about women and tax but got distracted by other issues.
He ended the interview and turned to Moylan:

Costello: Judi, are you coming?

Moylan: We were going to talk about women and tax.

Costello: I don't think they're interested.

MALE MEMBERS OF MAITLAND COUNCIL

To General Manager, Rhonda Bignell:

You're putting a good man out of a job.

PETER REITH,
FEDERAL MINISTER FOR INDUSTRIAL RELATIONS

The MUA will do anything to support its rorts, even put women in the front line.

JOHN HOWARD, PRIME MINISTER

Attempted to eliminate the gender-neutral term 'chairperson'
from Commonwealth bodies.

MYER DEPARTMENT STORE

Tried to keep women and non-whites out of its annual Santa school, saying Myer wanted to:

... protect the traditional authentic characterisation of Santa Claus ...
Myer takes its responsibilities regarding Santa Claus seriously.

MIKE GIBSON, MEDIA COMMENTATOR

Reasons against female Santas:

How many women, besides East German athletes, have long flowing beards?

DOM LOPEZ, MOSMAN COUNCILLOR

What would you know about business—you're only a housewife.

DAVID OLDFIELD, NSW ONE NATION MP

I certainly used to bring a little comfort to the lonely but now I don't have time.

BRUCE RUXTON, RETURNED SERVICES LEAGUE

Asked during a vote to install a woman as deputy chair of the Constitutional Convention:

Mr Chairman, what's gender balance?

1999
pearls before swine

The 1999 Ernies celebrated the 30th anniversary of the 1969 Equal Pay decision and, because 30th anniversaries are celebrated with pearls, the theme for the night became 'pearls before swine'.

The dress code was fittingly prescribed as 'posh frock and pearls'. This revealed a previously unknown fetish among Australia's feminists for pearls. The best display was from Eva Cox and Virginia Spate, who looked like old fashioned burlesque queens resplendent in ropes and ropes of pearls. They of course won the frock-off as judged by style icon Maggie Alderson.

The previous year, we received complaints that the awards ceremony had taken place in front of portraits of the Queen and Prince Philip. We'd simply been too busy to remember to take them down. This year they were removed at the last minute, leaving two ugly blank spaces on the wall. A search of the office came up with two suitable replacements: Tony Lockett and Che Guevara.

We had tried to organise the Trade Union Choir to sing, but they either refused to or did not know the words to: 'You Picked A Fine Time to Leave Me Lucille' and 'Stand by Your Man'. So we had to make do with recordings.

Women who nominated men were now known as dobbers. Competition for the Clinton was strenuous, with both Piers Akerman and Alan Jones being nominated for their entire oeuvre. John Howard was eliminated because he had won it the year before.

In the Elaine category there was a spectacular boo-off for the honour between Babette Francis and Jocelyn Newman, with the crowd chanting, 'Bab-ette, Bab-ette' or 'Joce-lyn, Joce-lyn'. Jocelyn won not so much for the quality of her remark as for the irony that she was the Minister for Women.

David Oldfield was nominated for his reflections on his relationship with Pauline Hanson in an article headlined, 'Sure, we talked about sex, but we were on a mission'. However, we couldn't work out which category it should be in.

Publican Susie Carleton presented the Gareth Award, as one commentator said, 'because she was the only woman sober enough to do it'. We cheered her story about her telling a diner at her famous pub who complained about being served by a pregnant waiter to 'Eat somewhere else, f . . . face!'

The raffle raised money to buy a cow for the Nelson Mandela Peace Village in Rwanda, which was run by widows of both Hutu and Tutsi men who had been killed during the genocide, and the winner won the naming rights for the cow. It was raucously and unanimously called 'Ernie'.

The Ernies went global in 1999 with the BBC waiting on the phone for the outcome of the Gold Ernie. Unfortunately a quote from *Debrett's New Guide to Etiquette and Modern Manners* had to be eliminated because it was not Australian. But here is it: 'It is bad manners to expel any liquid from any orifice in public, and breastfeeding is no different.'

Like the Oscars, everyone had an opinion on who should have won. Predictably, Paddy McGuinness wrote, 'Perhaps I will set up a new set of awards to be known as the Merediths for examples of biased, ideological and stupid feminism. There will be an all female jury.'

BILL LEAK, CARTOONIST FOR *THE AUSTRALIAN*

ABC RADIO NATIONAL
Axed *Women Out Loud* because:
There wasn't a need to have a specific women's program any more.

QUEENSLAND YOUNG LIBERALS
Called for on-the-spot fines for women who breastfeed in public.

JEFF KENNETT, VICTORIAN PREMIER

Talking to school girls:

Our women are not producing enough offspring to simply maintain our population levels . . . that's important to you [the girls] . . . it is important that we keep our population increasing . . .

JOHN LAWS, MEDIA IDENTITY

If she's done nothing else with her life, Monica Lewinsky has brought the entire women's movement to its knees.

P.P. MCGUINNESS, FAIRFAX COLUMNIST

But some of the most intelligent [feminists] are slightly crazy (like Germaine Greer), and some wimminists are just plain stupid. And it is true that some of our best-known feminists have slept their way to the top.

PETER COLEMAN,
THE FATHER OF PETER COSTELLO'S WIFE, TANYA

Tanya is a contemporary professional woman . . . She is a feminist—not the extreme, bra-burning lesbian type—but a women's rights feminist.

JOHN ELLIOTT, VICTORIAN BUSINESSMAN

While coming on heavy to a woman journalist,
he asked a male colleague who tried to intervene:

Do you own this woman?

NICK FARR-JONES,
FORMER WALLABY AND TRADITIONAL FAMILY MAN

If [my wife]Angie said go and unpack the car, I'd get pretty narky.

JOHN LAWS, MEDIA IDENTITY

*It would be cruel to say that the reason there are so few female
politicians is it's too time-consuming to make up two faces.*

P.P. MCGUINNESS, FAIRFAX COLUMNIST

*Female columnists seem unable to stop talking about either
their knickers or their cats, or their glass ceiling.*

BRAD NORINGTON,
JOURNALIST AND JENNIE GEORGE'S BIOGRAPHER

*They also know, based on [Jennie] George's highly emotional temperament, that her
agitation is likely to become a crescendo over the next year and that, backed by an
adoring party sisterhood, she had the potential to make life most uncomfortable for them.*

'MAGISTRATE NO 1'

In a case reviewed by the Judicial Commission:

Women cause a lot of problems by nagging, bitching and emotionally hurting men. Men cannot bitch back for hormonal reasons, and often have no recourse but violence.

'MAGISTRATE NO 2'

In a case reviewed by the Judicial Commission said to a woman who was assaulted for coming home late one night:

If you come home under those circumstances, what do you expect.

JOHN LAWS, MEDIA IDENTITY

On the leader of the NSW Liberal Party:

Kerry Chikarovski could boost her image a bit by hoisting the hem on her skirts a bit higher.

MICHAEL THOMPSON, POLITICAL WRITER

Working mothers with children are the cause of many problems in society ... this perception is consistent with a statistical correlation observed between female employment and serious crime rates.

ROTHMANS INTERNATIONAL

Cigarette advertisement

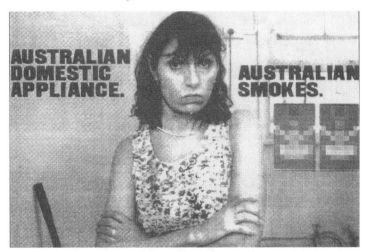

MCDONALD'S

An advertisement for Big Macs:

Me and the Big Merino
Me and the Big Pineapple
And a picture with his wife . . .
. . . That's the big mistake . . .

Skip the bikinis, forget the pasties: let's have nude volleyball and see how it rates.

CRAIG CARRACHER, VOLLEYBALL AUSTRALIA

Explained that wearing tiny bikini bottoms was
'value-adding' to the sport of women's beach volleyball:

The fact that we look good on TV is great.

EMILIYA MYCHASUK,
SYDNEY MORNING HERALD COURT REPORTER

The soft hennaed coiffure of the judge who turned 68 on Tuesday belied her often tough stance on many aspects of legal debate.

AARNE TEES,
NSW BARRISTER AND FORMER NSW DETECTIVE

Explained that his client, Romeo Nasr, had used a
stolen credit card to buy perfume because:

He's a Romeo by name and Romeo by nature . . . he fell into the clutches of a female and all that perfume was for her.

ROBERT RABBIDGE, CAMPBELLTOWN MAGISTRATE

Dismissed charges against a man who head-butted his girlfriend in a pub:

You're obviously a man who the Australian community will, over the years, get enormous benefit from.

JOHN HOWARD, PRIME MINISTER

In our approach to issues that affect women, we have not sought flashy symbolism, we have not indulged ourselves in things like quotas . . . and have not been over-slavish about targets.

JEFF KENNETT, VICTORIAN PREMIER

To Lynne Kosky, an MP with two young children who
asked for parliament not to sit late at night:

*It's a bit rich to ask that the whole parliamentary procedure be changed
to accommodate your requirements, which were obviously there
when you voluntarily offered to serve.*

JOHN RICHARDSON, VICTORIAN LIBERAL MP

Told Ms Kosky to have:

a cup of tea and a nice lie-down.

MARTIN FERGUSON, FEDERAL LABOR MP

Said the ALP should not focus on special interest groups, like women:

Middle-class, tertiary-educated 'femocrats' speak only to and for their peers.

GREG CORNWELL,
SPEAKER OF THE ACT LEGISLATIVE ASSEMBLY

*Talking about special women's services . . . presupposes that there is a
disproportionate amount of the normal services that have been provided . . . to
men . . . Why are we having special services for women and not . . . for men?*

ROBERT HO,
LABOR CANDIDATE FOR LORD MAYOR OF SYDNEY

Kathryn Greiner is a woman. She is not strong enough to be Lord Mayor.

SENATOR RICHARD ALSTON,
MINISTER FOR COMMUNICATIONS

Complained about the lesbian characters on the TV soap, *Breakers* because they were 'not normal', comparing them to left footers:

Normal kicks are right footed.

2000

even when she was fat

The eighth annual Ernie Awards celebrated the 25th anniversary of International Women's Day. The dress code was 'feathers and fur' (faux for the faint-hearted). The themes had no relation to one another except for jokes about feminists as endangered species. If you didn't have feathers or fur, the style police would allow anything except live pets.

The awards ceremony could have ended up being in very bad taste because the original Ernie had died that week, and his funeral had taken place the day before the big night. Well known SNAG and tactful journo David (Pembo) Penberthy pointed the finger at us: 'Mr Ecob may well have had the last laugh. He has left Sydney's feminists in the tasteless position of holding an event poking fun at him just twenty-four hours after his burial.'

'He probably timed it just to stick it to them one last time,' a male Labor MP added.

We decided to keep it tasteful and the only acknowledgment of Ernie's passing was the playing of 'Candle in the Wind' as the oblivious women entered the feasting hall. No other mention was made.

After criticism of our decision to replace the Queen and Prince Philip with Tony Lockett and Che Guevara, we decided to put our own portrait of the Queen in place of Prince Philip. It was a jazzed up version of Liz Taylor that evoked an eerie similarity to a young Princess Elizabeth.

In the weeks leading up to the Ernies we had been subjected to a stream of letters of abuse, pleading phone calls and anonymous nominations. From South Australia came a letter: 'As much as I would like to nominate several of my parliamentary colleagues, who over the course of the parliamentary session have often dismayed me with their inappropriate and bizarre comments, I am no good to anyone dead!'

A new category was added to accommodate the fast growing number of appalling comments by sports celebrities. The trophy for this category was a gold mobile phone known as the 'Warney'.

It was totally appropriate in the Olympic year that the Gold Ernie was won by Cathy Freeman's manager, Nick Bideau (or Nick *Bidet,* as the women hollered out), for what is still one of our favourite quotes. And Elaine Nile almost won the trophy named after her for this classic remark: 'I don't know how much I earn—I just give it to Fred and he puts it in an account.' Peter Reith continued an age-old Ernies tradition, blaming Ms X, the girlfriend of his son, for clocking up the dollars on his government credit card.

The raffle proceeds went to Jarrah House, a rehabilitation centre for drug dependent women and their children, and to PRADET, an organisation of East Timorese women involved in trauma counselling. The money was used to buy PRADET a sink and mirror so the women could 'wash and brush up at the same time'. The raffle prize was an Emily's List poster personally signed by Emily. Once again, Maggie Alderson immersed herself in the frock-off.

The following morning a number of journalists wanted to know whether D.D. McNicoll had won the media award. He had, and for the first time members of the media started seriously dobbing each other in.

However, the greatest thrill was that we were part of the *Sydney Morning Herald* crossword. On 2 October the clue for 25 across (5 letters) was 'Dingo could get an award', the answer of course being 'Ernie'. We had made it.

NICK BIDEAU,

CATHY FREEMAN'S EX-COACH AND EX-PARTNER

I never turned away from Cathy . . . no matter how
fat she was in 1997, or even in 1998.

SHANE WARNE, CRICKETER

If it had stayed private, it wouldn't have been a mistake.

WAYNE JACKSON, AFL CEO

I hope this doesn't sound sexist. It's not meant to be. Society is not ready to see females playing AFL football even if they are capable of doing it.

MICHAEL COSTA,
NSW LABOR COUNCIL SECRETARY (AGED 43)

On Sharan Burrow (aged 45) running for president of the ACTU:
She is just too old for the times.

HUGH MACKAY, SOCIAL COMMENTATOR

Younger women, in particular, have rejected the have-it-all-at-once approach of the early feminists and are typically more thoughtful than their mothers were in working out how to lead satisfying lives on their own terms. If only Greer had listened to some of them.

PETER REITH, MINISTER FOR WORKPLACE RELATIONS

Sent a delegation of twelve men to the ILO meeting
on maternity protection:
You don't have to be pregnant to present a policy position.

COLES SUPERMARKET

Their management training course identified pre-menstrual tension as:
a possible cause of workplace conflict.

KEVAN GOSPER, IOC DELEGATE

On his wife, Judy:
She is a trained corporate wife. She's a great asset.

DARRYL WILLIAMS, FEDERAL ATTORNEY-GENERAL

On why no women were appointed to the High Court:

*The government is very conscious of addressing the gender balance
on the Bench but as always appoints on merit.*

JASON YAT-SEN LI, REPUBLICAN MOVEMENT CAMPAIGNER
When Jodi Meares refused to launch the campaign T-shirts he said:
It's a shame. She had the chance to be the tits of the nation, but she's missed out now.

REV. FRED NILE, NSW CHRISTIAN DEMOCRAT MP
On the Olympic opening ceremony:
I'd say let's take 40,000 horsemen, something that shows Australians, a true reflection of Australia, its manhood. Not a lot of men dressed up as women.

GLAXOWELLCOME
Its flu treatment advertisement compared photos of two women, an unflattering one called 'Influenza' and a more flattering one called 'Common Cold', with the slogan:
You're more likely to go to bed with the one on the right.

JIM BEAM
An advertisement for cans of bourbon:
PUMP UP SALES. Grab a 6-Pack and get the girls.

JEFF CORBETT, *NEWCASTLE HERALD*
And reverse parking! Are women excused from doing a reverse park for their licence?

THE CHASER

A shameless self nomination for these headlines:

FEMINISTS SUCCESSFULLY RECLAIM NIGHT:
NOW TO RECLAIM MID-AFTERNOON

LIBERALS MEMBERSHIP DROPPING:
TANYA COSTELLO CALLED IN

SHAME: UK HUSSY STEALS WARNEY'S HOTEL KEY

D.D. MCNICHOLL, NEWS LIMITED COLUMNIST

Bradshaw left his team mates in the lurch so he could be by his fiancée's side while she gave birth . . . If the feminist plot of dads at births did nothing but take blokes away from work for a couple of hours, no one would complain. But keeping a key player away from a season final football match is an entirely different thing.

ANTHONY MUNDINE, RUGBY LEAGUE PLAYER

In an interview with *Lateline* about Stan Grant's affair with Tracey Holmes:

*AM: He's a great guy and I support him one hundred per cent.
He's done nothing wrong by his own culture.
Lateline: What do you mean when you say he's done
nothing wrong by his own culture?
AM: Well, polygamy. Aboriginal men are allowed more
than one wife, and he's done nothing wrong.*

JOHN HOWARD, PRIME MINISTER

To the captain of the victorious Australian netball team:

And I do want to say, on behalf of the government and everybody associated with the sport, what a tremendous ornament you have been, Vicki, to the game.

JOE DE BRUYN,
UNION OFFICIAL (AND INAUGURAL ERNIE WINNER)

Single women do not have a right to a child. They can't just say, 'I want it so therefore I should have it.'

MICHAEL LEUNIG, CARTOONIST FOR *THE AGE*

A poem suggesting it was better for university educated women not to have babies from the babies' point of view.
Again, Leunig exercised his right to refuse permission for the poem to be reproduced. As he said, he didn't want to risk 'more snide hostility from the mob'.

JOHN HOWARD, PRIME MINISTER

The issue [to stop lesbian couples and single women using IVF] involved overwhelmingly the right of children to have the reasonable expectation of the affection and care of both a mother and father.

DR JAMES HILTON, AUTHOR

On male DNA testing in sexual assault investigations:

It immediately presumed the assailant was a man,
yet women have been known to commit rape.

JUSTICE KENNEDY, COURT OF CRIMINAL APPEAL

On the first ever child-sex tourism case:

there was nothing to indicate the child had been an unwilling participant.

TOM PERCY, QC, NSW BARRISTER

Argued that six teenagers convicted of gang-raping a
young woman should not be jailed because:

they acted in accordance with the prevailing culture of the racing industry.

ROB KERIN, DEPUTY PREMIER OF SOUTH AUSTRALIA

. . . to help address some of the issues involved, for example,
domestic violence . . . and in some cases, serious crime.

THE *GOLD COAST BULLETIN*

The man threatened her with a knife, threw her to the ground and raped her.
While the woman was deeply shocked and traumatised, she was not injured.

RON CASEY, BROADCASTER

*If it's just a tap, like you give your wife when she doesn't have
dinner on the table on time, it doesn't count.*

DR MICHAEL WOOLDRIDGE,
FEDERAL HEALTH MINISTER

On why tampons should not be exempt from the GST:
As a bloke, I'd like shaving cream exempt but I'm not expecting it to be.

CHARLIE LYNN, NSW LIBERAL MP

*I'm not happy about someone else having my credit card details.
It's bad enough that my wife has them.*

2001
ernies to undies

The ninth annual Ernie awards invitation declared that in the centenary of Federation the theme would be 'Damned Whores and God's Police'. 'If you don't have an appropriate outfit, the style police (separate to God's police) will allow just about anything (except tacky PVC and inappropriate use of the Bible).'

The theme proved that, like Alexander Downer, all feminists will get into fishnet stockings at the drop of a hat. The author of *Damned Whores and God's Police*, Dr Anne Summers, judged the frock-off. Nuns' habits and feather boas cavorted through the hallowed halls of Parliament House but the eventual winners were the Marrickville Methodist Ladies Club in suitably 'temperance garb'.

Sekai Holland, who was well known to many of us as a leading figure in the anti-apartheid movement in Australia in the 1970s and is now president of the Women's Clubs in Zimbabwe, spoke with such passion about the poverty and deaths in Zimbabwe that we raised a record amount of money in the raffle. That money went to provide food in areas of Zimbabwe deliberately deprived of aid by President Mugabe.

Consultant Mark Patrick, with previous form in the Ernies, streaked the field in the media category with this comment: 'While a simple sleeveless shift dress is a must for any woman's wardrobe, sleeveless is a bad look, especially for anyone over thirty.' Probably because sexism segues so effortlessly into ageism, the women just hated this remark, and as reported in 'Sauce' in the

Sydney Morning Herald, 'This prompted some risqué behaviour on the part of the presenter, actress Judy Nunn . . . Nunn received a rousing applause for shedding her blouse and while striking a Charles Atlas pose in her black bra pointed to her now sleeveless getup saying, "I'm 56 and I think the man's a dickhead."' Extra poignancy was added by the fact that Judy Nunn's character on *Home and Away*, the beloved Ailsa, had just carked it on national TV.

The Elaine was overwhelmingly awarded to Pru Goward once again, this time for launching a line of cosmetics shortly after being appointed Federal Sex Discrimination Commissioner.

In the wash-up to the 2001 Ernies, when not a single male unionist had been nominated, union leader Alison Peters wrote: 'I refuse to believe that there are so few union men deserving of nomination. Let's see a return to the origins of the Ernies and ensure a union man gets the Gold.' Go Alison.

The winner of the Gold Ernie, however, was very concerned. Secondary Principals Association Deputy President Chris Bonner, who won with his comment 'The feminisation of the teaching profession sends a clear and unbalanced gender message to boys that they don't have to take education seriously,' claimed the quote was a compilation of other people's remarks and therefore he didn't deserve the award. So we took him to lunch, decided he was a good bloke and then in a historic boo-back awarded the Gold Ernie to John Howard for saying there was 'no appropriate woman to be governor-general.'

The 'Spike' column in the *Sydney Morning Herald* also objected to its nomination for displaying 'a gratuitous picture of women in bras.' It was just a week before the Ernies so 'you would think someone could have warned us,'

'Spike' wrote. To make amends 'Spike' printed 'a gratuitous picture of a bloke' with the caption, 'Do men really get offended by a picture of some bloke in his undies?'

MARK PATRICK, SYDNEY IMAGE CONSULTANT
Sleeveless is a bad look on many Australian women, especially those over thirty.

JOHN HOWARD, PRIME MINISTER
Said there was *'no appropriate woman'* for governor-general.

DON BURKE, CELEBRITY GARDENER
To singer Wendy Matthews in a segment about her garden:
So the biological clock . . . ticking away? What do you plan to do about that?

PETER BLACK, NSW LABOR MP
To the leader of the Opposition, Kerry Chikarovski:
Why don't you get a face-lift!

ALEXANDER DOWNER, MINISTER FOR FOREIGN AFFAIRS
Blew kisses and made obscene gestures across the Chamber to
opposition MP Julia Irwin. Downer said she was 'flattering herself'
if she thought they were directed at her.

RON BEST, VICTORIAN NATIONAL PARTY MP
*[Minister Gould's] breasts are so small that her front is
indistinguishable from her back.*

IAN CAMPBELL, LIBERAL SENATOR
When asked about Dame Beryl Beaurepaire's support of
the UN anti-sex discrimination protocol said:
*Australians in the suburbs will give the UN the two fingers, and I think
most of them would give Dame Beryl the two fingers as well.*

DAVID OLDFIELD, NSW ONE NATION MP
*She [fiancée, Lisa Johnston] has everything a feminist would admire except her
attitude towards men and families. She doesn't feel as a lot of women do, that
she has been cheated simply by having been born a woman.*

CAMERON WILLIAMS, FOX SPORTS PRESENTER
Said he needed to see his colleague's breasts to get him:
pumped for the show.

P.P. MCGUINNESS, FAIRFAX JOURNALIST
*It is especially objectionable coming from Justice Mary Gaudron, who
sometimes seems to forget that she was appointed to the court as a distinguished
jurist, not as an advocate for old-fashioned '60s feminisim.*

DAVID ETTRIDGE, ADVISER TO PAULINE HANSON

*In the early days I suggested to her if she was more demure
in her appearance and wore neutral colours like navies and whites
it would have a broader appeal to people rather than being
so distinctive in the bright florals.*

JEFF FENECH, FORMER WORLD CHAMPION BOXER

*I don't care what anyone says, we all may be equal, two arms and two legs,
but ladies aren't as tough as men, they can't take punishment the way a
man can. And I don't think it's ladylike to fight.*

JOHN ELLIOT, VICTORIAN BUSINESS MAN

When being breath tested, snatched the policewoman's
notes and called her 'girlie'.

THE *NORTHERN STAR*

The headline to a story about a preselection ballot between two women:

CAT FIGHT IN RICHMOND

ANTHONY MUNDINE, BOXER

*It's a warrior's sport. Men are warriors not women . . . boxing is a dangerous
sport and it is not right that women should box—leave boxing to men.*

IMRE SALUSINSZKY, *SYDNEY MORNING HERALD*

On the ALP affirmative action policies:

ALP ABILITY TEST: JUST FLASH US A BIT OF SKIRT, DARLIN':
But why 20 per cent in the first place? Surely taking their cue from the
Paralympics the comrades are capable of developing a more accurate
arithmetic of disadvantage than that.

CHIVAS REGAL

The billboard featured a woman (from the bust down)
in a mini skirt and the slogan:

Yes, God is a man.

And God created man and woman...

...but unfortunately, man got into advertising and things went downhill from there.

Wilcox

MARK MENTHA, ANSETT ADMINISTRATOR
On the airlines bankruptcy:

It's like going away on holidays on your own and coming back and asking your wife why you haven't got any money in the bank.

FRANK DEVINE, OPINION WRITER

The ABC's underdogs, whom it strives to liberate, are they minority groups such as women?

PETER JENSEN, ANGLICAN ARCHBISHOP OF SYDNEY

For biblical and historical reasons, I oppose having women bishops and believe they would create great difficulties for communion and fellowship ... Women should not be the elders or priests in a congregation.

P.P. MCGUINNESS, FAIRFAX COLUMNIST

The inevitable push for paid maternity leave will have a devastating impact on the employment market for women ... if the whole burden of this is to be thrust onto business and onto male employees in business, there will be an inevitable backlash.

SHANE WARNE, CRICKETER

I am from the old school where the men bring home the bacon and the women look after the home.

HAMISH MCLAUGHLIN, MEDIA COMMENTATOR

Most polo players think that their horses are more valuable than wives.

JOHN WATKINS, NSW MINISTER FOR CORRECTIVE SERVICES

*Be proud of your husbands, sons and brothers as they go
off to work in their Corrective Services uniforms.*

PAT CASH, TENNIS COMMENTATOR

*Look at Lindsay Davenport. She's a big girl. When you look at her, you think, whoah,
there is no way she is going to be a tennis player. Put her in the shot put instead.*

2002
will it be the willy?

The 10th Ernie Awards celebrated the 100th anniversary of women's suffrage in NSW. The dress code was appropriately green, white and violet, the colours of feminism and the secret code of the suffragettes—GWV for 'Give Women the Vote'.

The ceremony was held amidst controversy over the 'Good Ernie' for Boys Behaving Better. With the revelation of Gareth's affair with Cheryl Kernot, it was decided to junk the name the 'Gareth'. The only male we could think of who was totally perfect in all ways was the former governor-general, Sir William Deane, but the award would then be known as 'The Willy'. This predictably engendered childish sniggers so the now nameless trophy was simply referred to as the 'Anon'. There was also some argument that the sports trophy, the Warney, should be renamed the 'Waynie' after philandering footballer Wayne Carey.

A new trophy had to be found for the burgeoning 'Clerical' section. Once again the paucity of choice at sports trophy shops resulted in the selection of a giant leaping marlin, the fish representing Christianity. The inaugural winner was the Pell Pot of Australian Catholicism, Archbishop Pell.

Val Buswell, stalwart of the War Widows' Guild and Business and Professional Women, nominated NSW National Party MP Andrew Fraser for telling a female minister to 'go and wash up' during a parliamentary speech on the difficulties faced by women in small business. As Val said, 'At his age he should have more sense.' And at 80, she'd know!

Women from all around Australia continued to send in comments made by men in their organisations. In 2002 we received a deluge of complaints about local councillors.

Singer Little Pattie, AKA Patricia Amphlett, presented the media award. We implored her to leave early to save her voice for the 'Long Way to the Top' concert the next night, but to the horror of other baby boomers also bound for the concert, Little Pattie stayed booing loudly well into the night.

The raffle proceeds went to RAWA, an Afghan women's organisation providing education for girls.

We were thrilled to discover a serious academic article which referred to the Ernies as 'an articulation of opposition'. We weren't quite sure what it meant, but we sure celebrated.

And the Ernies were once again international news. A toffee BBC reporter asked, 'What is it that makes *Australian* men say these things?' And we had to *defend* Australian men. Imagine that! He obviously thought that only in a faraway colonial outpost would these terrible things be said.

There was also a very serious and very accurate report in the *Malaysian Star*. What the good citizens of Kuala Lumpur felt about our Archbishop receiving an award for sexism was not recorded.

And Labor MP Joel Fitzgibbon let it slip that Mark Latham had rung him from Germany to find out what he had been nominated for. We were certainly keeping the men nervous.

RAY HADLEY, BROADCASTER

On Germaine Greer at sixty-three:

I bet she's now sorry she burnt her bra all those years ago.

TONY ABBOTT,
FEDERAL MINISTER FOR WORKPLACE RELATIONS

A bad boss is a little bit like a bad father or a bad husband—notwithstanding all his faults you find he tends to do more good than harm.

SIR ALBERT ABBOTT, NATIONAL PARTY STALWART

On De-Anne Kelly, Federal National Party MP:

She's a good candidate – for a woman.

ANDREW BOLT, *HERALD SUN*

Nobody said or imagined that a court would use this vague and silly law [the Sex Discrimination Act] to extend IVF to lesbians and (worse) single mothers.

JASON AKERMANIS, AFL PLAYER

No. 4 is too attractive to be a hockey player.

ABC TV SPOKESPERSON

On why the live broadcast of an Australia vs New Zealand netball
test match was cut four minutes before the end:

But New Zealand were going to win anyway. It wasn't that close.

WARREN BROWN, *DAILY TELEGRAPH* CARTOONIST

ANDREW FRASER, NSW NATIONAL PARTY MP

Told the NSW Minister for Small Business, Sandra Nori, to:

Go and wash up!

And then defended himself by saying he would never be sexist because:

My life is governed by those of the fairer sex,
including my wife and my two secretaries.

WAL KING, LEIGHTON'S HOLDINGS CEO

On donating to both political parties:

If you don't do it, there's a chance of getting a black mark against your name.
It's like giving your wife flowers – why wouldn't you do it?

THE HIGH COURT OF AUSTRALIA

Justifying its decision to cut a young woman's compensation payout
by 20 per cent for her husband's accidental death:

A woman of her age and circumstances would be likely to remarry,
making her less in need of compensation.

IAN CALLINAN, HIGH COURT JUDGE

On the same judgment:

Judgments like these are made. You don't have to
put people in bathing suits to make them.

DAVID PENBERTHY, NEWS LIMITED JOURNALIST

On relaxing rules on the photographing of MPs in the chamber:

Perhaps the best way to do it is to just pick one MP ... let's make it Sophie Panopoulos ... and just take heaps of pictures of her. She is kind of pretty. She would probably look great when angry.

RICK DAMELIAN MOTORS

Advertising a car sale:

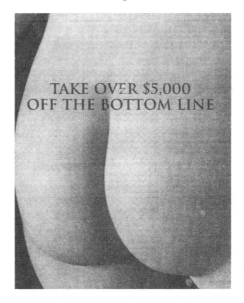

TAKE OVER $5,000
OFF THE BOTTOM LINE

ALAN RAMSAY, FAIRFAX COLUMNIST

Described Democrats leader Natasha Stott Despoja as 'little Natasha' and said:

[The Democrats are] a disintegrating babble rabble presided over by a young woman far out of her depth who has no business being taken seriously.

SYDNEY MORNING HERALD

Headline for a story about a TV debate between women politicians:

CLAWS IN AS WOMEN POLITICIANS FEEL THE STUDIO HEAT

'SYDNEY CONFIDENTIAL', *DAILY TELEGRAPH*

SPOTTED . . . actor Lisa Hensley pulling off a spectacular three-point turn followed by an amazing reverse park.

WAYNE CAREY, AFL PLAYER

Made excuses for having sex with his team-mate's wife, saying:

She followed me into the bathroom. In front of everyone.

THE AUSTRALIAN

Promoted on the front page a special report on:

WHY FATHERS MAKE THE BETTER SINGLE PARENT

GLENN DAVIES, ANGLICAN BISHOP OF NORTH SYDNEY

I don't believe that headship by a woman is part of God's way. The head of a congregation is like the head of a household . . . it should be male.

KENNETH HACKETT,
HACKETT LABORATORY SERVICES DIRECTOR

Said being forced to sign a union agreement was: *like being raped.*

DICK WARBURTON, DAVID JONES CEO

Said he was: *unable to find a woman of sufficient talent to join the board.*

RODNEY ADLER, FAI DIRECTOR

I wanted to pass FAI on to my son.
(... and not one of his three daughters?)

GEORGE PELL, CATHOLIC ARCHBISHOP OF SYDNEY

Abortion is a worse moral scandal than priests sexually abusing young people.

IAN CAUSLEY, FEDERAL NATIONAL PARTY MP

After Labor MP Nicola Roxon made a speech on child sexual assault:
I thought for a while you were calling for volunteers, Nicola.

DR PETER HOLLINGWORTH, GOVERNOR-GENERAL
On allegations of the sexual abuse of a 14-year-old
girl by an Anglican Minister:
*There was no suggestion of rape or anything like that, quite the contrary.
My information is rather that it was the other way round.*

NICK MINCHIN, LIBERAL SENATOR
On maternity leave for working women:
*It reeks of more middle-class welfare and it means
non-working mothers are being discriminated against.*

TONY ABBOTT,
FEDERAL MINISTER FOR WORKPLACE RELATIONS
Compulsory paid maternity leave? Over this government's dead body.

MARK LATHAM, FEDERAL LABOR MP
Described women as: *just an interest group.*

JUSTICE RODDY MEAGHER, NSW COURT OF APPEAL
*There are so many bad ones that people may say that women can't be good
barristers and are hopeless by nature – it's a pity the able people don't come.*

DARYL WILLIAMS, FEDERAL ATTORNEY-GENERAL

On appointing more women to the bench:

It may be possible in the near future to make further inroads particularly in relation to the Federal Court, without compromising on the quality of appointment to the Bench.

JON PHILLIPS, PENSIONER

Unsuccessfully sued the NSW Attorney-General for harm inflicted on him by up to 100 women in government departments:

I don't have an adverse attitude to women, except those who are bitches, including my ex-wife.

After forty years, she had clearly had enough and left him:

She took all the furniture except the marriage bed. When I woke up in the morning the first thought I had was, 'Who's going to get my breakfast?'

MR ANGRY'S IDEAL WOMAN...

2003
hairy legs and tufty armpits

The 11th annual Ernie Awards took place in the Parliament House dining room as usual wedged (timewise) between a Girl Guides lunch and the alcohol summit the next morning. Some would say auspicious timing.

The dinner celebrated 20 years since the first New South Wales woman was elected to Federal Parliament, and 20 years since Australia ratified the United Nations Convention on all forms of discrimination against women and also, to many of us, the very important anniversary of 30 years since Billie Jean King defeated Bobby Riggs in the famous 'Battle of the Sexes'.

To convince those from the dark side (anti-sport) that sport was important in the fight for women's rights, we read out this description of the match: 'The Battle of the Sexes captured the imagination of the country, not just tennis enthusiasts. On 20 September 1973 in Houston, Billie Jean was carried out on the Astrodome Court like Cleopatra in her gold glitter held aloft by four muscular men dressed as ancient slaves . . .' We even wrote to Billie Jean asking her to be a guest presenter at the occasion. We assured her that we were celebrating not only her victory, but also her campaign for equal pay for women tennis players—a constant Ernies theme, thanks to sports writer Jeff Wells.

The dress code was 'Wimbledon Best (on or off court) or anything Damir Dokic would disapprove of . . . '.

And for the first time the invitation allowed women to tick the appropriate box for catering choices 'vegetarian', 'vegan' or 'greedy'. We had to discontinue this as all the women ticked 'greedy'.

Tables for the occasion were named after wicked women including Typhoid Mary, Lorena Bobbitt, Lizzie Borden, Bloody Mary, Jezebell, Anna Nicole Smith, Rose Porteous—you get the picture.

This was the year that celebrity chefs almost equalled sporting stars in their misogyny. As the clerical nominations of previous years had dried up, that category was changed to 'Culinary'. Fortunately, the fish trophy could accommodate both.

Warney himself continued the great Ernies tradition of blaming everything on women. He claimed his mum gave him that diuretic tablet.

The frock-off consisted of endless women in Wimbledon outfits looking more like Margaret Court than Anna Kournikova, along with a couple of butch truck drivers. It was judged by Jeannette McHugh, the woman whose election to Parliament twenty years before we were celebrating. Jeannette 'I don't know enough about frocks' McHugh did a sterling job.

Once again, the raffle proceeds went to the Zimbabwean women and to the National Pay Equity Coalition to produce a leaflet on what the changes to the IR laws would mean for women's wages.

Ernie try-hard Jeff Corbett of the *Newcastle Herald* wrote 'If my making the short list is a guide there will be 400 pairs of hairy legs and tufty armpits booing over dinner, not to mention some very blubbery midriffs, and no Ernie could match that spectacle for sexism.'

The following day the Treasurer of NSW, Michael Egan asked Parliament, '. . . the real question is whether I got an Ernie. If not, why not?'

RON CASEY, BROADCASTER

On Victorian MP Kirsty Marshall breastfeeding in Parliament:
A second rate politician with a first rate publicity stunt. I mean, how else could a member of the Lower House of the Victorian State Government get her name and boobies splashed all over the national press?

BRIAN PEZZUTTI, NSW LIBERAL MP

To two women MPs:
I love it when you two toil and bubble and interject. Talk dirty to me. Come on, talk dirty to me. I love it . . .

DAMIR DOKIC, JELENA DOKIC'S FATHER

More than 40 per cent of women in world tennis are lesbians. I couldn't stand it if Jelena turned out to be one of them. I'd kill myself.

JOHN HOWARD, PRIME MINISTER

Real marriage is for the continuation of the species.

NEIL PERRY, CELEBRITY CHEF

Doesn't every woman want to get married? Don't they grow up dreaming of it?

CHRIS CONDON, PROPERTY DEVELOPER

I've done wrong things by women something shocking.
But I've never done anything dishonest.

IPEX ITG

Sacked a woman who had severe morning sickness,
writing to her while she was in hospital:
We have no choice but to conclude that you have abandoned your employment.

STELLAR CALL CENTRE

Docked the pay of a pregnant woman because she
took too many toilet breaks.

BRISBANE TATTERSALLS CLUB MEMBER

If we allow women in we won't be able to swear and fart and scratch our balls
... When it comes down to it there is nothing wrong with a boys' club.

BRENDAN SMYTH, ACT MP

One of the areas that is quite interesting is the number of women who,
having had an abortion, engage in greater risk-taking behaviour ...
There is evidence to suggest that it may even lead to a
greater number of women in prison.

JUSTICE RODDY MEAGHER, NSW COURT OF APPEAL

Most of them [public housing tenants] were foreigners and many of them were female.

NEIL PERRY, CELEBRITY CHEF

On Nigella Lawson's TV cooking show:

Why doesn't she just get 'em out; that's what they're watching for!

VAUGHAN JOHNSON, QUEENSLAND NATIONAL PARTY MP

Sponsored the Hog 'n' Dog wet T-shirt competition.

JOHN BRODGEN, NSW OPPOSITION LEADER

To Premier, Bob Carr:

Sit down, you stupid girl!

JOHN HOWARD, PRIME MINISTER

Claimed that paid maternity leave as a solution
to balancing work and family was:

intellectually insubstantial.

NICK MINCHIN, FEDERAL FINANCE MINISTER

Said paid maternity leave was:

dangerously naive and a waste of time and taxpayers' money.

JUSTICE RODDY MEAGHER,
NSW COURT OF APPEAL

If you find a woman who is No. 1 in the merit list, of course she should be appointed, but there is no such person.

DAVID BORGER, MAYOR OF PARRAMATTA

On the push for women candidates in the Labor Party:

A whole generation of young guys has been locked out. There's never been much merit in selection processes—now there is none. A generation of young men are being told they need not apply.

PETER MOXHAM, WARRINGAH COUNCIL

Called the Local Government Women's Conference:

a feel-good motherhood talkfest we have from time to time.

GEOFF CLARK, PRESIDENT OF ATSIC

Thanked the Aboriginal women who voted for him for president, saying:

You've given us a mandate. You've returned the traditional role to Aboriginal men.

PAUL GIBSON AND **MATT BROWN,** NSW LABOR MPS

Auctioned Kylie Minogue's undies as a fundraiser.
When Kylie reacted angrily, Matt replied:

I know they're real. If Kylie calls me, we can sort this out.

JOHN LAWS, BROADCASTER

Called Kelly Osbourne:

a witch of a woman and a foul-mouthed little slut.

MARK LATHAM
Called opinion writer, Janet Albrechtsen:
a skanky ho.

STEVE PRICE, BROADCASTER
Called a female journalist:
a stupid little bitch.

ALAN RAMSAY, FAIRFAX COLUMNIST
Called veteran political commentator, Michelle Grattan:
the gallery's ageing blue heeler.

ANDREW BOLT, *HERALD SUN*
. . . women are more likely to act irrationally . . .

PETER TAYLOR, MENTONE BOWLS CLUB
*Ladies don't want to play against men. They don't want bowls whistling
around their ankles. They can't get out of the way quick enough.*

GREG NORMAN, GOLFER
On Annika Sorenstam entering a men's golf tournament:
For Annika's sake I hope she doesn't get hurt.

STEVE LIEBMANN, CHANNEL NINE

Said that getting Justin Madden to say 'Go the Pies' was:

like a woman having to say sorry.

HARRY GIBBS, FORMER HIGH COURT CHIEF JUSTICE

*It is true that there are some very able women in the legal profession,
but it is no disrespect to them to say that none has the learning,
ability and experience of Justice Heydon.*

A *HOBART MERCURY* JOURNALIST

When interviewing an oncologist:

*Is it because you're a bloke that you're interested in
breast rather than testicular cancer?*

JEFF CORBETT, *NEWCASTLE HERALD*

*When we see a young woman with an exposed belly we think, how revolting is
that? At an age when girls should be striving to be pleasing to the male eye, these
young women were going to serious lengths to expose an acre of wobbling excess.*

DAVID HOOKES, VICTORIAN CRICKET COACH

In defence of Shane Warne:

Some dopey hairy-backed sheila has dobbed him in on the other side of the world.

ROGER ROGERSON,
DISGRACED FORMER NSW DETECTIVE

Ian David is a boof-headed, bald-headed c... I should have sued the c... and those f...wits at the ABC, but of course I've got no credit left.

SHANE WARNE, CRICKETER

I can confirm that the fluid tablet I took before appearing to announce my retirement from one-day cricket was given to me by Mum.

DARREN LEHMANN, CRICKETER

Sledged a Sri Lankan cricketer *Black c****

JEFF WELLS, FAIRFAX SPORTS WRITER

Some women are better than some men.
But at the top men are better. End of story.

2004

mobile phones are weapons of mass destruction

Yet again, the timing of the 12th annual Ernie Awards was awkward. As the hopeless bunch of ageing feminists and career-girl-wannabes traipsed into the Parliament House dining room, we found lying on the tables the menu from the previous function, an 'Achieving Women' luncheon featuring radio broadcaster Sally Loane and a number of Liberal women Members of Parliament. We momentarily felt inadequate, until the champagne kicked in and the booing started.

The 2004 Ernie Awards celebrated the 20th anniversary of the Federal Sex Discrimination Act and 100 years (and 13 days) since women first cast their vote in a New South Wales State Election. We also discovered that it would have been veteran feminist Edna Ryan's 100th birthday, so we had plenty to celebrate.

Inspired by a year of rugby league scandals, including the totally inappropriate way in which Canterbury Bulldogs players dressed as they entered a police station for questioning over allegations of sexual assault, we decided that the theme for the evening was 'team bonding' with an 'inappropriate' dress code—'thongs and stubbies are OK.' We were expecting Willie Mason wigs (we got them), and of course fishnet stockings and one disgustingly behaved Reg Reagan.

Determined not to miss another bad taste moment, we played 'Candle in the Wind' as the women arrived. Not for the original Ernie this time, but rather in memory of Ernie all-time great, cricketer David Hookes.

The Warney was the most hotly contested category, assisted by the 2003 ruling that SMS messages were valid nominations. Unfortunately many of those nominations were too rude to quote here, but they certainly caused much outrage on the night. In the great Ernies tradition of blaming women, Pat Cash was nominated for blaming Delta Goodrem for the Scud's poor form.

There were very few nominations in the Judicial category. We claimed victory!

The Anon trophy for Boys Behaving Better was still without a name. We did vote on naming it the 'Goodes' after Sydney Swans player Adam Goodes who took his mum to the Brownlow dinner and called her his inspiration. (We love blokes who are nice to their mums.) But the vote was aborted—we kept losing count, and the trophy remains nameless.

The crowd was encouraged to embrace the theme 'to indulge in binge drinking and texting something obscene to someone you have just met'.

The frock-off was to be judged by Ian 'Dicko' Dickson but he didn't turn up. As the theme was 'inappropriate', the only possible winner was the magnificent Patricia O'Brien, AKA the Duchess of Redfern, in her Great Aunt Peg's fox fur complete with paws, teeth and beady glass eyes.

The raffle raised money for the Alola Foundation, which was established by East Timor's First Lady, Kirsty Sword Gusmao, to address violence against women and girls in East Timor. Xanana Gusmao sent us a personally signed book of his poems for first prize.

Ownership of local heroes and villains was shown by the *Manly Daily* which trumpeted 'Peninsula men have figured in the annual Ernie Awards— but at opposite ends of the spectrum', Tony Abbott for being bad and Sea Eagles captain Michael Monaghan for being good.

We were subject to a vicious attack by Janet Albrechtson in *The Australian* who somehow thought that our naming of the Repeat Offenders award after Bill Clinton meant we approved of him. She still does not believe the only invitation criteria for the Ernies function is a frock and a sense of humour.

On the other hand the man who has probably gained most from the Ernies, going from 'nobody' to 'Ernies Stalwart', Jeff Corbett, not only sent us his column about the Ernies in advance but wrote: 'Hope you have a lovely time tonight, company withstanding.'

MALCOLM NOAD, BULLDOGS RUGBY LEAGUE CLUB CEO
On allegations that Bulldogs players raped a woman in Coffs Harbour:
Let's believe nothing happened in Coffs Harbour.

DARREN LOCKYER, AUSTRALIAN RUGBY LEAGUE CAPTAIN
Joked about the assault allegations and the name of league great Johnny Raper:
You know, St George, they won eleven premierships with one Raper,
imagine how many Canterbury are going to win.

GEOFF CARR, AUSTRALIAN RUGBY LEAGUE CEO
Said Lockyer's 'Raper joke' would have no bearing
on the Australian captaincy because:
We can't expect our players to be diplomats 100 per cent of the time.

MARK GASNIER, ROOSTERS RUGBY LEAGUE PLAYER
Left this message on the phone of a woman he had just
met while out on a 'team bonding' night:
*There's four toey humans in the cab—its 20 to four. Our ... are fat and f ...
ready to s ... s ... and you're in bed. F ... me—fire up, you sad ...*

JOHN ELLIOT,
FORMER CARLTON FOOTBALL CLUB PRESIDENT
On the AFL taking action against the culture of
footy players preying on women:
*Asking all girls for the last twenty years that have had any problems to
write in is one of the most profoundly stupid things I have seen ...
it's not going to help the football club, and it won't help some
of the players that may have been involved.*

EDDIE MCGUIRE,
COLLINGWOOD FOOTBALL CLUB PRESIDENT

I'm saying there is [sic] as many predator women [as men] these days, whereas once upon a time that may not have been the situation. There are absolutely as many predator women, I mean, I've spoken to our guys about it and they tell me.

MELBOURNE FOOTBALL CLUB

Told Club Vice-president Beverley O'Connor not to attend an official club function because the atmosphere would resemble that of a 'stag night'.

PAT CASH, TENNIS COMMENTATOR

Blamed Delta Goodrem for Mark Philippoussis' poor form:
It looked like he was up all night doing whatever . . . getting busy. It's the stuff off the court that's proving distracting for him.

PATRICK FITZGERALD, *CRIKEY* SPORTS EDITOR

Usually I find watching women's tennis about as appealing as watching darts. You know they're good—but who cares?

CRAIG PARRY, GOLFER

When questioned about Laura Davies playing in a men's tournament:
What do you want—political correctness or what I really think?

MARK BOSNICH, SOCCER PLAYER
On allegations he beat his girlfriend:
She was attacking me . . . I told her, I'll throw you out naked . . . I chucked her bags out into the hall . . . apparently an ambulance came and took her away.

CRAIG JOHNSTON, VICTORIAN UNION OFFICIAL
I'm obviously upset that my many supporters have wrongly gained the impression that I'm a big girl's blouse, scared of doing some time.

A MEMBER OF THE UNION CLUB, SYDNEY
On why he voted to keep women out of the all-male club:
I do not want my lunch interrupted by the likes of Bronwyn Bishop or Jennie George.

ALAN JONES, TALK-BACK RADIO HOST
I have a view that people ought to decide for themselves who should be members of their clubs. If they don't want to have women, well, who cares?

WESTCO CLOTHING STORE
Insisted that female staff wear T-shirts with the slogan:
Stop pretending you don't want me.

When female staff complained management said:
The T-shirt must be worn . . . No T-shirt equals no work.

P.P. MCGUINNESS, FAIRFAX COLUMNIST

The crude abuse coming from many of the ageing feminists and their ideological children who have for years repeated the tired old stuff about women having the sole rights over their own bodies . . . merely shows that they have devoted no serious thought to the issue since the 1970s.

JOHN HOWARD, PRIME MINISTER

Boasting about the number of women in his ministry (six out of thirty-six):
It's all been done without the patronising use of quotas.

ROD CAMERON, POLLSTER

Said Labor's women's policy was:
The last gasp of the ageing femocrats who still delight in having a women's policy. It's being done for form only, to keep the Joan Kirners and the Anne Summerses happy. It doesn't cut any ice in the wider electorate.

'SYDNEY CONFIDENTIAL', DAILY TELEGRAPH

Described socialite Maria Venuti as:
Maria 'with the hooties' Venuti.

JOHN MARSDEN, CHILDREN'S AUTHOR

Teenage boys are among the most maligned groups in our society.

JOHN HOWARD, PRIME MINISTER

Vetoed the $20 million campaign against domestic violence
because it was too 'anti-male'.

STEVE PRICE, BROADCASTER

Called the *Daily Telegraph*'s gossip writers 'two dopey sheilas':
*[their column] is written for girls aged between fifteen and twenty-five
and that's about the intelligence of the people who must read it.*

PETER WEST, ACADEMIC WRITER

*I recognise problems as soon as I enter the staffroom . . . when the wedding
photos come out, or Tupperware parties are discussed, there isn't much for most
men to relate to. No wonder men under thirty-five years of age are leaving
the profession faster than anyone else.*

ANDREW BOLT, *HERALD SUN*

*If your sex is a factor in getting you your job, sex will still be
counted a factor when you do that job badly.*

AUSTRALIA POST

Told female staff at the Bondi Junction office to lose weight if they
wanted to attend the opening of the new post office.

TONY ABBOTT, FEDERAL HEALTH MINISTER
Abortion in Australia has been reduced to a question of the mother's convenience.

DAVID PENBERTHY, NEWS LIMITED JOURNALIST
I know when I'm being threatened and did the only manly thing. I panicked like a girl.

IAN 'DICKO' DICKSON, *AUSTRALIAN IDOL* JUDGE
To idol contestant Paulini Curuenavuli:
Choose more appropriate clothing or shed a few pounds.

GORDON RAMSAY,
BRITISH CELEBRITY CHEF VISITING AUSTRALIA
On a former girlfriend:
Going to bed with her was like having a rottweiler strapped to your chest.

LUKE MANGAN, CELEBRITY CHEF
On Princess Mary:
She's got some natural class about her. She's not one of those Aussie bimbos.

IAN HARRISON, PRESIDENT OF THE NSW BAR ASSOCIATION
Justifying the lack of senior women lawyers:
*Advocacy is at its purest form an intellectual exercise where
hormones and chromosomes have no relevance.*

JOHN HOWARD, PRIME MINISTER

Argued against a paid maternity leave scheme because:

It would not increase the fertility rate or improve job security.

ANDREW BARTLETT, FEDERAL DEMOCRATS LEADER

Drunkenly manhandled Liberal Senator Jeannie Ferris and called her:

a f...ing bitch

PETER BLACK, NSW LABOR MP

Drunkenly lunged at Strathfield MP Virginia Judge during the liquor licensing debate. No one could actually understand what he said.

RICHARD ALSTON,
FEDERAL MINISTER FOR COMMUNICATIONS

Blamed his mum when accused of a conflict of interest over Telstra shares.

PHILIP RUDDOCK, FEDERAL ATTORNEY-GENERAL

Proposed changing the Sex Discrimination Act so that all-male teaching scholarships could be offered without any corresponding offers to women.

TONY SHAW, COLLINGWOOD AFL COACH

The team presented like body-builders but played like they wore dresses.

BRENDAN NELSON,
FEDERAL MINISTER FOR EDUCATION
On the Sex Discrimination Act:

It will do this country no good if we spend the next decade hand-wringing and clinging to misplaced but well-guided ideological purity.

PETER WEST, ACADEMIC WRITER

Male voices in classrooms are hugely different; they're louder and deeper. Many of my students say that their boys and girls come home from school saying joyfully: 'Mum, I've got a man!'

MARK LATHAM, FEDERAL OPPOSITION LEADER

For boys without men in their lives this is a real issue: a lack of male mentors and role models teaching them the difference between right and wrong.

JOHN HOWARD, PRIME MINISTER

The Labor Party places a greater priority on not changing a single comma in the Sex Discrimination Act than it does in helping boys who need a male role model.

BRENDAN NELSON, FEDERAL MINISTER FOR EDUCATION

In New South Wales, 250 government primary schools have not got a single male teacher. Scary stuff.

MARK SKELSEY, *DAILY TELEGRAPH*

Sydney parks are being turned into barren lifeless dustbowls by dogs and women. That's right, dogs and women . . . Now Sunday is women's soccer day and as a result, our poor parks are being chopped to death by the 'over-35s North Shore mums' competition.

TOOHEYS

'MAL THE BLOKE' COLUMN, *DAILY TELEGRAPH*

Women who claim they 'love to watch sports' must be treated as spies until they demonstrate knowledge of the game and the ability to drink as much as the other sports-watchers.

GRAEME EDWARDS, FEDERAL LABOR MP
Called Veteran's Affairs Minister Danna Vale:
a flip flop floozy.

STEVEN CONROY, FEDERAL LABOR MP
Called colleague Nicola Roxon:
a skanky ho.

FRANK SARTOR, NSW MINISTER FOR ENERGY
*I think [Opposition Leader] John Brogden gets screeching and hysterical . . .
maybe he's got a female side.*

MAL BROUGH, FEDERAL MINISTER FOR DEFENCE
On women fighting in frontline combat:
*Our concern is that the operational effectiveness and capability
of the defence force not be compromised.*

JUSTICE RODDY MEAGHER, NSW COURT OF APPEAL
Described a portrait by a woman artist as:
*. . . a touch too pretty and feminine, but better than the usual academic
rubbish which passed muster in Sydney portrait painting circles.*

STEVE PRICE, BROADCASTER

Kate Langbroek should not have brought her baby to work and breastfed on air.

PAUL REYNOLDS, MELBOURNE BARRISTER

To a client's breasts:

Just let me feel those puppies then, they're beautiful.

SHANE WARNE, CRICKETER

In a text message, of course:

How bout we meet up in the toilets?

2005
the ernies model

The 13th annual Ernie Awards celebrated the 30th anniversary of International Women's Day and the 30th anniversary of no-fault divorce. The theme was: 'BLING: We know you've got it so we expect you to wear it'. Shockingly, a number of women had no idea what 'bling' was and were outed on the night. They were urged to get a life and read more women's magazines while waiting in the checkout line at the supermarket.

The press reported that 400 women, two brave men (first and last time) and a baby attended on the night. There were 86 nominations, not quite a record field, but pretty good. Once again we had to eliminate a ripper of an international quote with Jude 'It's Sienna's fault I cheated' Law continuing the wonderful tradition of blaming everything on women.

Judicial figures were better, celebrity chefs were better and the Reverend Fred Nile (after whom the Clerical/Celebrity/Culinary trophy the 'Fred' is named) was nominated for saying he never goes into a room alone with a woman. We are still not entirely sure why.

Sporting stars were still bad. There was even a discussion about whether Shane Warne should be permanently disqualified because he blitzes the field every year. Luckily there was very strong competition from Australian rugby league player, Willie Mason.

We were all sure that Derryn Hinch would win the Media Silver Ernie for his appalling comments about Schapelle Corby but, no, Dave 'Sluggo' Richardson from *Today Tonight* came through with a beauty.

The Elaine produced an absolute surprise winner, Colleen McCullough. The crescendo of booing which greeted her extraordinary remark showed once again that the most bile is reserved for the Elaines.

The awarding of the Gold Ernie to Sheikh Feiz Mohammed was a worry. He was certainly a worthy winner but we were afraid that we would be subject to a fatwah. We were therefore very relieved when the Good Ernie went to Islamic activist Keysar Trad.

Brendan Nelson's scathing quote about universities and maternity leave, which won him the political Silver Ernie, prompted a very serious article in *Arts Hub Australia*, 'His statement characterises paid parental leave as a wasteful extravagance on the part of VCs and Nelson reveals the low priority given by this government to work/family balance issues.' It was nice to see our night of fun having a serious effect.

The frock-off was to be judged by Paris Hilton, but she was unavoidably detained in a video store. So Patricia O'Brien, still wearing her Great Aunt Peg's fox fur from the previous year, covered for her. She ignored the dress code and gave it to Deb Jopson's mum for her beautifully appliqued hat.

The Ernies led to two quirky but important sidelights in 2005. The Plain English Foundation wrote to us asking for advice on how to run a successful awards night: 'The Ernie awards are a model for us. We want our awards to be equally successful and would much appreciate any pointers.' And our ACT chapter invented 'The Gregs', named after their own favourite sexist, former ACT politician Greg Cornwall. Their winner was rugby league chief executive Geoff Carr, for his response to the furore over Darren Lockyer's 'Johnny Raper' joke: 'We can't expect our players to be diplomats 100 per cent of the time.'

WILLIE MASON, BULLDOG'S RUGBY LEAGUE PLAYER

All I have done was to go out with the New South Wales team,
drink a heap of piss . . . We didn't do anything out of the ordinary of
other bonding nights . . . there were a lot of allegations . . .
but who gives a shit mate, we won the comp.

RICKY PONTING, AUSTRALIAN CRICKET CAPTAIN

Matt [Hayden] is one of the best chefs I've ever known.
I still don't know why he got married.

ERIC RUSH, FORMER ALL BLACK (ALMOST AUSTRALIA)

In the old days, you were a good guy if you lifted
your feet when she was vacuuming.

TONY ABBOTT, FEDERAL HEALTH MINISTER

On Mary Donaldson and every little girl's dream of marrying a prince:
Every time one person's dreams come true the world is a better and brighter
place for all of us. Your marriage was a gift to the people of Australia.

STEVEN GIBBONS, FEDERAL LABOR MP

To Veterans' Affairs Minister De-Anne Kelly:
I suppose a rort's out of the question?

RODDY MEAGHER, RETIRED NSW JUDGE

*Looking at the shrivelled old parsnip Germaine Greer has
now become, I can hardly believe she was the comparatively
beautiful young woman I once knew.*

DAVE 'SLUGGO' RICHARDSON, CHANNEL SEVEN

Ambushed a woman in a carpark armed with a hidden camera:

Sluggo: How many kids have you got?
Mary-Anne: five
Sluggo: How many dads have you got?
Mary-Anne: Oh, I don't want to do this, thank you, no...
Sluggo: How many, darling?
Mary-Anne: No...
Sluggo: How many, darling?

JIM COURIER, AUSTRALIAN OPEN TENNIS COMMENTATOR

Pointing at commentator, Johanna Griggs:

Who's that blonde bimbo?

When John Alexander listed Grigg's considerable achievements,
Courier replied:

So I'm supposed to be impressed?

PAT CASH, TENNIS COMMENTATOR
On Bec Cartwright:
Hey, she's up the duff.

JOHN BROGDEN, NSW OPPOSITION LEADER
To Minister Diane Beamer:
We are not in a classroom, love.

JOHN DORIS, NSW BARRISTER
Commented during a child prostitution case:
*These girls [aged thirteen & fourteen] . . . are not like nice little nieces
from a good school. They were accustomed to deception.*

ROLF DRIVER, FEDERAL MAGISTRATE
Ruled that forcing a woman to wear a miniskirt at work was not
sexual harassment because the woman:
admitted owning short skirts and wearing them socially.

BRENDAN NELSON,
FEDERAL MINISTER FOR EDUCATION
Attacked the university vice chancellors for offering paid maternity leave
while still needing money for other services.

TONY ABBOTT, FEDERAL HEALTH MINISTER

Are people being railroaded into [having abortions] by parents, husbands and boyfriends and the culture of convenience?

MAJOR GENERAL MICHAEL JEFFERY,
GOVERNOR-GENERAL

I believe, basically, that the best form of family is Mum, Dad and the kids. That's the fundamental.

JOHN BROGDEN, NSW OPPOSITION LEADER

Explained while judging the Miss East Coast Girl contest
at the Newport Arms Hotel that:

When judging a contest you look for intelligence, humour, an ability to speak well publicly . . . Oh yes, looks play a part too.

ROSS CAMERON, FEDERAL LIBERAL MP
Once said:

It's incontrovertible that two-parent households provide social and economic benefits, both for the family itself and for the community more generally.

But after being caught cheating on his wife admitted:

If my constituents want to vote for a great family man they should probably vote for the other guy. (... who was a woman!)

His campaign slogan was alarmingly honest:

JOHN HOWARD, PRIME MINISTER
When he found out that Liberal MP Ross Cameron had cheated on his wife, said:

He told me he was going to run again and I wanted him to do that because he's been a very hard working local member.

LEN HARRIS, ONE NATION SENATOR

If you did a comparison between Pauline Hanson and Len Harris, starting from the ground up, she wins hands down in the legs department. She has a body that would launch a thousand ships. Mine would sink them.

MAJOR GENERAL MICHAEL JEFFERY,
GOVERNOR-GENERAL

Declared that the number of terminations in Australia each year was too high:
That's as many as our immigration quota.

IAN HARRISON, QC, NSW BARRISTER

While cross-examining a teenage victim in a pack-rape case said:
To sit on a bar stool . . . with a skirt as short as that takes a lot of confidence.

SOUTH SYDNEY PRESBYTERIAN CHURCH SPOKESPERSON

Women should learn in quietness and full submission.

PHILLIP JENSEN, ANGLICAN DEAN OF SYDNEY

Called Anglican evangelicals who accepted women's ordination:
mealey-mouthed and able to be domesticated.

GEORGE PELL, CATHOLIC CARDINAL

On the ordination of women priests:

Not in any lifetime!

SHEIKH FEIZ MOHAMMED, NSW ISLAMIC CLERIC

A victim of rape every minute somewhere in the world. Why? No one to blame but herself. She displayed her beauty to the entire world ... strapless, backless, sleeveless, nothing but satanic skirts, slit skirts, translucent blouses, miniskirts, tight jeans ... to tease man and appeal to his carnal nature.

TREVOR CORKER, WINE MARKETING MANAGER
For women, wine is not an intellectual pursuit.

ANTHONY WARLOW, SINGER
On being overwhelmed at a business women's lunch:
The noise! I have some chickens at home that sound similar.

MICHAEL, *BIG BROTHER* CONTESTANT
Thought that rubbing his penis in Gianna's hair without
her knowing was *'just a practical joke'.*

RODNEY ADLER, FAI DIRECTOR
Said he likes his wife to have his children bathed and fed and
his dinner on the table when he comes home:
It would also save a lot of time if she could chew my food.
But sadly I have to do that myself. As awful as that may sound,
that's exactly the way it is and exactly the way I like it.

A *BIG BROTHER* SOURCE
On former *Big Brother* contestant, Hotdogs:
Anyone who's watched the show knows full well he's got a healthy appetite
for women. And after being quarantined for so long, it is now dinner time.

VIRGIN BLUE

Rejected the applications of women aged over 36 for
flight attendants jobs and promoted the airline with this image.

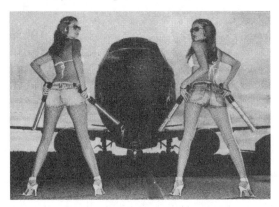

FHM MAGAZINE

*Branson has brought the sexiness and panache back into air travel. While
Qantas keep with their fang-toothed wenches and bearded coffee witches on the
payroll, the girls of Virgin have given new meaning to the phrase, 'Hot towel, sir?'*

JOHN SINGLETON, RADIO STATION OWNER

On his new female station manager:
*It's still harder for birds to make it, especially when they're not ugly.
If she was fat and ugly it probably wouldn't be a problem.*

MIKE O'CONNOR, *COURIER-MAIL*

On swimmer, Lisa Curry-Kenny:

The neckline plunged impressively into a deeply tanned cleavage, looming out of the winter gloom and parting waves of cardigan and coat-clad workers before its significant thrust.

MICHAEL DUFFY, FAIRFAX COLUMNIST

On Mark Latham's decision to withdraw from politics:

Ignoring or suspicious of other males and surrounding himself with supportive women, his mother, his wife and sisters . . . You wonder if things might have been different had the loner been able to talk to other men who might have put his problems in a less domestic context.

JOHN LAWS, MEDIA IDENTITY

Yes, but that doesn't bother selfish little bitches who just get themselves pregnant and then decide they don't want the child. They don't care about anybody else.

TOM LLOYD, PUBLISHER OF THE *NORFOLK ISLANDER*

On the rape trials on Pitcairn Island:

Having a few of those early Tahitian genes still circulating in my body I can't see how anybody could be charged with rape when after all, they were only doing what comes naturally.

RAY CHESTERTON, NEWS LIMITED WRITER
On colleagues Anita Quigley and Amanda Platell:

I wouldn't mind if the girls used Cinderella as a role model, especially the early days when she was doing the housework . . . At least a man would stand a chance of having his desk dusted and getting the odd can of Coke delivered.

JOHN LAWS, MEDIA IDENTITY
About *Queer Eye for the Straight Guy*'s Carson Kressley judging the Melbourne Cup Race Day fashions:

He was judging the girls, now what the hell does a pillow biter know about judging girls? They should have had a few truckies down there, or me.

P.P. MCGUINNESS, PADDY'S MEDIAPACK WATCH
On ABC radio announcer Sally Loane:

Poor old Sally, [she] starts imitating the Radio National's appalling **Life Matters** *program, with Women'ith [sic] chit chat about nappies, kiddies, orgasms for elderly ladies or what have you. It's a* **Women's Weekly** *for ladies with degrees, no ideas and nothing useful to do.*

MIKE COLMAN, *DAILY TELEGRAPH*

Women's wrestling came to the Olympics yesterday . . . There's not a vat of jelly in sight and the only shaving cream is in the competitors' dressing rooms (no five o'clock shadows allowed) . . . It would be unfair to describe [wrestler] Stavroula as masculine. Unfair and dangerous . . .

DERRYN HINCH, MEDIA IDENTITY

Schapelle Corby has been getting all this attention because she is young, white, pretty and has big boobs.

2006

four hundred of Australia's
most powerful women

The 14th Ernie awards celebrated the 20th anniversary of the establishment of the Human Rights and Equal Opportunity Commission and also 30 years since early Ernie contender and baseball writer Dan Cook coined the phrase, 'The opera ain't over till the fat lady sings.'

The dress theme was 'Opera Diva', so women were invited to 'come as your favourite opera singer or doomed heroine'. Valkyrie horns and flaxen plaits abounded. And yet again more fishnet tights, this time on women presumably trying to look like Carmen. The frock-off was judged by Dame Jenny Macklin, who unlike the women in fishnet tights behaved perfectly at all times.

The Welcome to Country was performed by Gamilaroy Elder Rosemary Curtis, the first Indigenous woman on Glen Innes Council.

With the theme of the 'fat lady singing' we had to broach the delicate issue of whether this would be the last Ernies, as Parliament would no longer be our home. However, we promised the women that the opera ain't over just yet and that 'the book' would appear in 2007.

There were a record number of nominations in all categories, including a terrific haul of fifteen nominations for the Good Ernie. We also started receiving abusive emails, including one from a well known male newspaper editor: 'Who've you got to f . . . to get a nomination for an Ernie? People are beginning to talk about me'. He knows who he is.

The tradition of blaming women was taken a step further by Justice Marcus Einfeld who blamed his speeding fine on a dead woman.

The greatest response of the night was reserved for the presentation of the Good Ernie to Gough Whitlam for his comments about how the number of women in parliament influenced the RU486 debate for the better. Guest presenter of the award Little Pattie burst into a chorus of 'It's Time'. 'It was an absolute highlight,' the *Sydney Morning Herald* reported. 'Everyone reckons the hair stood up on the back of their necks.'

Once again we managed to gain international media coverage, including the 30 August edition of *The New Light of Myanmar* Vol. XIV No. 136.

However, the most significant events of the 2006 Ernies occurred after the ceremony. Bill Heffernan rang our office several times and proceeded to tell whoever answered that:

(a) he was delighted to have received his award, and

(b) what he said about Julia Gillard was true; he was an old farmer and he knew about 'heifers and bulls and rams and ewes'. He somehow felt that this made his comment perfectly justifiable.

But the really amazing story of 2006 resulted from the awarding of the Celebrity Silver Ernie to Tom Cruise for his 'I've got Katie tucked away . . .' quote. After a long debate during our stringent credentialling process we decided that Tom could be classed as an Australian because of his (previous) 'Australia's favourite son-in-law' status. Tom's win was reported widely in Australia and overseas including on *Fox News* America: 'Four hundred of Australia's most powerful women have just voted Tom Cruise not the *sexiest* but the most *sexist* celebrity in the world.'

His subsequent denial was also reported worldwide. The *San Francisco Gate* wrote, 'Hollywood superstar Tom Cruise has denied he made a comment that won him the Ernie award for most sexist celebrity in Australia last Thursday.' His representative Arnold Robinson said, 'Anyone who knows him knows that he is a complete gentleman and would never ever say such a thing.'

Editor of *Who* magazine Jane Nicholls rang to say that Tom (who was a bit under the pump at the time because of his sofa-jumping and weird Scientology exploits) was very upset. We answered that the Ernies always demanded high standards of authentication and stood by our source, which was ABC Online, and even if he didn't say it he should have been nominated for his attack on Brooke Shields for taking medication for postnatal depression. We also offered to discuss it over a lamb roast.

This was reported back in America and two days later, guess what, Tom Cruise apologised on national television to Brooke Shields. The tentacles of the Ernies are everywhere.

TOM CRUISE, AUSTRALIA'S FORMER FAVOURITE SON-IN-LAW

*I've got Katie tucked away so no one will get to us until my child is born . . .
her life from now on is going to be about being a mother—I'm not giving
her the chance to turn into another Nicole.*

MEL GIBSON, ACTOR

What do you think you're looking at, sugar tits?

MICHAEL 'ASHLEY' COX, *BIG BROTHER* CONTESTANT

Said he should not have been thrown out of the *Big Brother* house for the
turkey slapping incident because he 'did nothing wrong'.

ADAM BOLAND, *SUNRISE* EXECUTIVE PRODUCER

*There is something about female journalists that says they'd
just walk over dead bodies to get the story.*

MIKE CARLTON, MEDIA IDENTITY

On Camilla Parker-Bowles:
The Duchess of Cornwall is the current Protestant whore.

BILL HEFFERNAN, FEDERAL LIBERAL MP
On Labor MP Julia Gillard:

Anyone who chooses to deliberately remain barren . . . they've got no idea what life's about. We've got a few on our side as well.

She should have children. And if she did have them, she shouldn't be pursuing a career in politics—she should be at home, looking after them. Julia Gillard is a barren, neglectful mother!

ALEX MITCHELL, *SUN HERALD* JOURNALIST
On Irene Moss, ICAC Commissioner and partner of Macquarie Bank's CEO running for the Sydney University Senate:

Let it go, Irene, and just stay home counting the money or knitting.

RAY HADLEY, BROADCASTER

Claimed 'reverse discrimination' when a Sydney hotel asked his friends to vacate a function room for a lesbian event:

It was fairly obvious these young ladies were lesbians because they were holding hands and they dressed like men.

JEFF CORBETT, *NEWCASTLE HERALD*

On the space shuttle Discovery, which was commanded by a woman:

The other woman among the crew of seven was an engineer, but NASA ensured there was a male engineer on board in case things went wrong.

THE *SUNDAY TELEGRAPH*

SERENA WILLIAMS ON *THAT* PICTURE: I WAS SHOCKED BY MY OWN SIZE

THE AUSTRALIAN
GRANDMOTHER TAKES SEAT ON HIGHEST COURT

THE *DAILY TELEGRAPH*
WIN FOR WOMEN IN LEGAL FIRM CAT FIGHT

'SYDNEY CONFIDENTIAL', *DAILY TELEGRAPH*
Quoted Pamela Anderson saying: 'I have a very addictive personality'
and then commented:
which might explain Pamela Anderson's big hooters.

ZOO WEEKLY MAGAZINE
In an interview with singer Nikki Webster:
Nikki Webster: I want to stay true to myself. It's all about progression.
Zoo: Have your boobs gotten bigger?

TED ROBINSON, ABC TV
On why he gave Julie McCrossin a job:
She juggled her boobs at me in a non-sexual way but could not be denied.

'SYDNEY CONFIDENTIAL', *DAILY TELEGRAPH*

The great battle of the women's mags continues this month with New Woman *giving away a 'one size fits all' bikini with each issue. We might get our mate Maria Venuti with the hooties to test that theory.*

UNILEVER

When questioned about the way the Lynx deodorant 'Get on, get off' advertisements depicted women, a spokesman explained:
The whole campaign is about fantasy and the representation of women is consistent with that.

'SYDNEY CONFIDENTIAL', *DAILY TELEGRAPH*
STORM IN A DD CUP FOR MARIA

GRANT BIRSE, NETBALL AUSTRALIA
Said ABC TV commentator Anne Sargeant was:
old and detrimental to the game.

RICHARD HINDS, *SYDNEY MORNING HERALD*
*Jana Pittman now had a gold medal and Tamsyn Lewis
only the chest on which to pin it.*

PIERS AKERMAN, NEWS LIMITED COLUMNIST
*There is no doubt that the [Labor Party's] misguided practice of positive
discrimination in favour of lacklustre minority candidates, both women
and members of ethnic groups, in the faint hope of currying factional favour,
has been disastrous for the nation.*

SHANE WARNE, CRICKETER
*I've had a few one-night or two-night stands or whatever you want to call it . . .
I've never fallen in love with anyone.*

EDDIE MCGUIRE, CHANNEL 9 CEO

Asked as he plotted to sack newsreader Jessica Rowe:

When should we bone her? I reckon it should be next week.

HUGH MACKAY, SOCIAL COMMENTATOR

There is an emerging sub-species of young female drivers—a grotesque mutation of the spirit of the pioneering feminists—who use bad manners, on the road and elsewhere, as a symbol of their independence . . . They'd rather die than graciously give way to another car, especially one driven by a man.

GARY NEIWAND, CYCLIST
Spied on his ex-wife and secretly urinated in a glass of
champagne which she drank. He said:
I'm happy, a happy man. I have got her out of my life.
I'm ashamed about nothing I do.

PHIL GOULD, RUGBY LEAGUE COMMENTATOR
I was at a coaching clinic the other day with a thousand kids and 940 of them
were doing the Benji Marshall step. The other sixty were girls but,
you know, at least they were giving it a go.

REX HUNT, FISHING SHOW HOST
On paying for sex:
I paid money thinking I would get confidentiality so I could protect my wife.

STAN KEKOVICH, FORMER AFL PLAYER
Why on earth did they dispatch text messages to English trollops when
plenty of Aussie sheilas would gladly target their middle stump.

DAVID LOWY, PBL DIRECTOR
You're only as old as the woman you feel.

DAVID BENNETT, QC,
COMMONWEALTH SOLICITOR-GENERAL

*Justice Susan Crennan doesn't come with baggage of any kind . . .
she is not a crazy feminist.*

ALLENS ARTHUR ROBINSON, LAW FIRM

Sacked two female secretaries over a heated email exchange about a missing
ham and cheese sandwich but did nothing about the male lawyers who
forwarded the email exchange to their friends around the world.

SOL TRUJILLO, TELSTRA CEO

*Of greater relevance [to women] is whether a Blackberry fits into a handbag,
whether the keyboard can be locked to prevent unintentional dialling from
knocking against sunglasses, and whether there's a choice of colours.*

JUSTICE PETER YOUNG, LAW BOOK CONTRIBUTOR

*. . . it is clear that some female solicitors have no idea of appropriate court dress.
The worst offenders are usually well-built women who expose at least the upper
halves of their breasts and as they lean forward to make a point to a judge
sitting on a higher level, they present a most unwelcome display of bare flesh.*

TOSSON MAHMOUND, TEACHER

Women should not be in any senior position over men. Nature does not mean it to be.

PETER WEST, ACADEMIC WRITER

Boys and girls learn better at school when they are listening to a male voice.

VIRGIN AIRLINE

Encouraged scantily clad cabin crew to pose for
FHM magazine with the headline:
Brace yourself for trouser turbulence.

SECURITY OFFICER, LOS ANGELES AIRPORT

Questioned Qantas Chairperson Margaret Jackson about
why she had aircraft plans and diagrams on her. When she said
she was the chair of an airline, he said:
But, you're a woman!

MALCOLM TURNBULL, FEDERAL LIBERAL MP

Emailed a constituent, saying:
*Gosh Pam, you are in a bad mood this morning. Now, you are correct that
the budget did not target childless, 58-year-old lesbian poets and science
teachers but you are better off nonetheless.*

P&O CRUISES

Advertised cruises with the slogans:

More Girls. More Sun. More Fun. There's nothing else a guy needs to know!

and

Seamen Wanted!

PETER BEATTIE, PREMIER OF QUEENSLAND

Ms Bligh is Deputy Premier and Treasurer and every
other piece of shit I don't want.

LEN KIELY, NORTHERN TERRITORY MP

Said to a woman security guard who refused him a drink:
*I have a very long tongue and I could use it on you and
make you a very happy woman.*

THE YOUNG LIBERALS

Disrupted a National Union of Students Conference, chanting:
We're racist. We're sexist. We're homophobic.

JOHN BROGDEN, NSW OPPOSITION LEADER

When asked what the future held for retiring Premier Bob Carr replied:
Well, he can ship his mail-order bride back on the boat.

PETER JENSEN, ANGLICAN ARCHBISHOP OF SYDNEY

Said he was disappointed at the election of Bishop Katharine Jefferys Schori:
not because of her gender but because of her reference to the 'Mother Jesus'.

REV. FRED NILE, NSW CHRISTIAN DEMOCRAT MP

On how to solve the Big Dipper roller coaster
noise problem at Sydney's Luna Park:
*The simple solution is to prohibit all females from using these machines. Engineers
have said the high pitched screams of females are breaking the noise levels.*

BILL LUDWIG, BALDING UNION OFFICIAL

Julia Gillard reminds me a lot of Bronwyn Bishop. It's all about the hair.

PETER COSTELLO, FEDERAL TREASURER

Have one for the husband, one for yourself and one for the country.

DAVID LECKIE, CHANNEL 7 CEO

Told female presenters to follow the 'jugs under chins'
approach to dressing for TV.

GORDON RAMSAY, BRITISH CHEF VISITING AUSTRALIA

*Women are better off mixing a gin and tonic than meddling with modern cuisine
. . . young women can't cook to save their lives.*

2007

uncovered meat

The year 2007 has proved to be a case of 'same old, same old'. The issue of women in the media bumping their heads against, not a glass ceiling, but a very sharp guillotine, was raised over and over again as 40-something women lost their jobs while ageing, balding men remained on screen. A parallel theme was that of career women ruining relationships.

'Hooters' made a spectacular entrance to the field when Silver Logie winner Aaron Jeffrey made his acceptance speech about *McLeod's Daughters* actors having the 'best boobs in the business'. He may well make Australian history by being the first person to do the double and win a Logie and an Ernie in the same year.

Bill Heffernan once again commented on Julia Gillard's suitability for political office, based on her insides, but probably the most enduring remark of the year came from Sheikh Taj el-Dene Elhilaly. His comments about 'uncovered meat' caused, as it should have, a huge controversy. From the Ernies perspective, however, the point must be made that clergy of all faiths in Australia have made remarkably similar comments over the years, and show equally misogynistic attitudes towards women.

With the Ernies ceremony yet to take place, we have no idea who will win the frock-off. Draw your own dress is probably the best instruction.

AARON JEFFREY, ACTOR

In his Silver Logie acceptance speech:

Cast and crew of McLeod's Daughters . . . there's some great actresses, definitely the best boobs in the business . . . makes coming to work every day very easy.

DANIEL MCPHERSON, ACTOR

The next Logie recipient:

I can't believe he just said that but he's right.

GORDON WOOD, DRIVER FOR RENE RIVKIN

To an astounded morgue attendant during the identification of his dead girlfriend, Caroline Byrne:

Do you mind if I look at her tits?

JOHN HOWARD, PRIME MINISTER

On the suitability of a semi-naked burlesque act at a government climate change conference:

I'm sensitive to the view of many women in relation to this but I do think we shouldn't overreact.

JOE HILDEBRAND, *DAILY TELEGRAPH*

This was based on the flawed assumption that girls have an innate talent for hairstyles in much the same way as they have an innate talent for buying shoes.

GRAHAM, FATHER OF FLIGHT ATTENDANT LISA ROBERTSON

Defended his daughter having mid-flight sex with
actor Ralph Fiennes, saying:
*The other flight attendants were probably as ugly as
a hatful of arseholes and were just jealous.*

CHANNEL TEN EXECUTIVES

Sacked forty-one-year-old news reader Tracey Spicer because they wanted to:
Freshen up the look.

'SYDNEY CONFIDENTIAL', *DAILY TELEGRAPH*

*Kate Fischer let it all hang out in an array of plunging numbers minus
the most important accessory: a bra. Someone tell her that pancakes
are best served with something over them.*

PAUL KENT, *DAILY TELEGRAPH*

On Germaine Greer:
*For everything else there seems to be someone younger, smarter and yes,
prettier, with opinions more worthwhile.*

ABC *BASTARD BOYS*

Portrayed the entire MUA/Patricks dispute without even one
appearance by ACTU President, Jennie George.

GERARD HENDERSON,
SYDNEY INSTITUTE MEDIA WATCH QUARTERLY
Commenting on TV news presenters:
Let's commence with the gorgeous, pouting Jacinta Tynan.

WARREN BROWN, *DAILY TELEGRAPH* CARTOONIST

THE *AUSTRALIAN WOMEN'S WEEKLY*
On a photo of Princess Mary taking her son to kindergarten:
Mary's mumsy hairstyle, jeans, plain shoes and brown overcoat raised many eyebrows.

TONY ABBOTT, FEDERAL HEALTH MINISTER
These days . . . for women who have got their whole lives ahead of them or women who have got things nicely under management—a baby, or an extra baby, is a terrible inconvenience.

KARL STEFANOVIC, TELEVISION IDENTITY
Joked that the woman with the winning bid in a charity car auction:
couldn't wait to jump in the back seat.

KYLE SANDILANDS, *AUSTRALIAN IDOL* JUDGE
Told *Idol* contestant Jessica Mauboy to:
lose the jelly belly.

PAUL KENT, *DAILY TELEGRAPH*
On Germaine Greer opening the door nude:
The sight of the 67-year-old in full glory, her flabby bits flapping intelligently in the wind, is something I wouldn't have survived.

JOE HOCKEY, MINISTER FOR WORKPLACE RELATIONS

Well, it's exhausting for me, her being pregnant . . . I don't know why, during the birth process they only focus on the women. What about the men standing there? I mean, that's pretty hard. Well, as long as they get the cricket in the hospital.

PAUL KEATING, FORMER PRIME MINISTER

I will not be harassed by journalists, even by pretty ones like you. Nick off.

MARK LATHAM, FORMER LABOR MP

Claimed that the Aussie bloke is in 'crisis' and has been replaced by:
. . . nervous wrecks, metrosexual knobs and toss bags . . . [because] . . . left-feminists have sanitised public culture . . .

CHRISTIAN KERR, *CRIKEY*

An industrial relations cat fight erupted on Saturday's AM between Heather Ridout of the AIG, and Sharan Burrow from the ACTU . . .

A BARKER COLLEGE OLD BOY

In 2006 the institution that has been the male First XI Barker team has been challenged, by a girl named Alyssa Healy. Clearly this is an attack that cannot be accepted. All ex-students must join in fighting this outrageous decision.

BILL HEFFERNAN, LIBERAL SENATOR

Said yet again that Julia Gillard was not qualified to lead
the country because she is 'deliberately barren':

I won't walk away from that . . . so rude, crude and unattractive as it was . . .
if you're a leader, you've got to understand your community.

JOE HOCKEY,
FEDERAL MINISTER FOR WORKPLACE RELATIONS

When asked why he's not as popular as the Shadow Minister, replied:

I'm not as pretty as Julia Gillard, obviously.

THE AUSTRALIAN

Headlined a story about tennis player Serena Williams:

AFTER BOTTOMING OUT, SERENA'S BACK

THE *DAILY TELEGRAPH*

Front page headline about a woman who abandoned
her newborn baby at a hospital:

**HOW COULD SHE:
The poor little baby dumped by her mother**

SUNDAY TELEGRAPH

SINGLE MUM = FAT KIDS

THE *DAILY TELEGRAPH*

CAN A CAREER WOMAN REALLY BE A GOOD WIFE?

TONY ABBOTT, FEDERAL HEALTH MINISTER

*I won't be rushing out to get my daughters vaccinated [against
cervical cancer], maybe that's because I'm a cruel, callow,
callous, heartless bastard but, look, I won't be.*

A SENIOR ALP LEFT FACTION FIGURE
Belittled the preselection nomination of seven
women for the Senate, saying:
*At the national conference dinner last month they went around and got
whichever woman was pissed enough to sign a nomination form.*

WARWICK CAPPER, FORMER AFL PLAYER
*Expectant father, Darren Jolly, needs to get his priorities in order.
The birth of your first child is special, but if you are a machine like me,
there's more children to be had than premierships.*

SIMON BENSON, *DAILY TELEGRAPH*
*Cartoonists Warren Brown and Bill Leak behave like
two old spinsters living together.*

BILL HEFFERNAN, LIBERAL SENATOR
Said priests should be permitted to marry because:
like the rest of us, they wake up with a horn at four in the morning.

WAYNE COOPER, FASHION DESIGNER
On Australian models:
compared to the runways in Europe, they're porky.

CHANNEL NINE

Advertised its cricket coverage with an ad featuring model
Lara Bingle playing cricket in a green and gold bikini.

PETER FARIS, QC, MELBOURNE BARRISTER

*I criticise the number of women being appointed. I am opposed
to affirmative action in judicial appointments.*

SHEIKH TAJ EL-DENE ELHILALY, MUFTI

On rape victims:

If you take out uncovered meat and place it outside on the street without a cover and the cats come and eat it...whose fault is it, the cats or the uncovered meat? The uncovered meat is the problem. If she was in her room, in her home, in her hijab, no problem would have occurred.

JOHN RICHARD HEATH, WRITER

Agreed with Sheikh Elhilalay:

Many Australian working-class women dress like tarts.

ANDREW JOHNS, RUGBY LEAGUE GREAT

F . . . you, c . . . !

JOHN SINGLETON, ADVERTISING GURU

Anyone who doesn't say f . . . and c . . . shouldn't be allowed to play rugby league.

JEFF CORBETT, *NEWCASTLE HERALD*

Words that specify size can be useful . . . as in 'Get a load of those gobstoppers!'
A few that are worth noting so we can bring variety to our exclamations
are whoppers, melons, coconuts, bazookas, mammoths and, not to
discriminate against the deprived, fried eggs. Hooters, too, is used for
big 'uns, although I'm not sure why.

the good ernie
previously known as the Gareth
and the Anon

This chapter is otherwise known as the very short chapter, or by some as the boring chapter. The Good Ernie tradition began in 1994 when a male trade unionist finally said something good about women.

We have been accused of inventing the Good Ernie simply as a sop to men. On occasion we have even been accused of awarding the trophy to prominent males as some sort of suck-up. None of these criticisms are true, but you just have to take our word for it. In fact we discovered that the women were genuinely thrilled when men behaved better.

There have been some problems with this award. The first and most obvious was the continual debate about the name. We've had to change its name from the Gareth to the Anon, and almost to the Willy but eventually it simply became known as the Good Ernie.

The other problem for the judges was that sometimes we felt that the nominees didn't really believe what they were saying. Did John Laws really mean it when he finally conceded that single mothers are single mothers because of relationship breakdowns?

To our surprise we discovered that a number of men appeared in both categories, the good and the bad, men such as Peter Costello, Mark Latham, Bob Carr and even Paddy McGuinness. We felt that when they do say something good we should recognise it, but perhaps it's just that they say so much that eventually something good has to pop out! However, like girls with curls, when they're good they're very, very good, but when they're bad they're horrid.

1994

PETER SAMS, NSW LABOR COUNCIL SECRETARY

On the National Pay Equity Coalition's submission to the
Review of Wage Fixing Principles:

*I found it well argued and supported by the evidence and
I wholeheartedly endorse its conclusions.*

1995

AUSTRALIAN MANUFACTURING WORKERS UNION

Ran a workplace campaign against sexual harassment.

1996

ERNIE PAGE, NSW MINISTER FOR LOCAL GOVERNMENT

Referred a local council to the Anti-Discrimination Board for overlooking
experienced women employees by not advertising to fill the Manager
of Library and Community Services position but instead giving the
responsibilities to the Manager of Sport Facilities because
'they didn't want to lose him'.

1997

PETER CAMERON,
FORMER PRINCIPAL OF ST ANDREWS COLLEGE

On university college boy songs:

What these songs do is degrade women to the level of beasts . . .
There seems to be almost a feeling that women have let the side down by
being female and not male and they are to be punished accordingly.

1998

ERNIE PAGE, NSW MINISTER FOR LOCAL GOVERNMENT

Sacked Maitland Council for sexual and physical harassment, saying:

Some of the evidence that has come to light about the conduct of the councillors
is disgraceful. One of the prime cases of gender prejudice and unacceptable
conduct has been the attitude and hostility to Ms Bignell
as general manager.

DR CRIS MCMAHON,
AUSTRALIAN CENTRE FOR SEXUAL HEALTH

On Viagra:

If someone reported that burying yourself in horse dung to your ankles
would make your erections better, people would do it.

1999

GEORGE TRUMBULL, AMP CEO

Invited ten senior women to lunch and got them to list
their ten most sexist male colleagues.

BRUCE MCAVANEY, SPORTS COMMENTATOR

*Should women tennis players get the same prize money
as the men? You bet they should!*

2000

BOB CARR, NSW PREMIER

On a woman's right to IVF regardless of sexual preference or marital status:
*Access to IVF should be a matter between a woman and her doctor . . .
there will be no change to our anti-discrimination laws.*

PETER FITZSIMONS, MEDIA IDENTITY AND AUTHOR

*. . . get Tiger Woods and Karrie Webb to play a Battle of the Sexes
golf game against each other . . . She's killed 'em on the women's
tour, he's killed 'em on the men's.*

2001

FOUR ATTORNEYS-GENERAL 🏆
MATT FOLEY, QUEENSLAND;
BOB DEBUS, NEW SOUTH WALES;
ROB HULLS, VICTORIA;
PETER PATMORE, TASMANIA

The Commonwealth Government is undermining our national reputation by refusing to sign or ratify the Optional Protocol to the Convention on the Elimination of All Forms of Discrimination Against Women.

ADAM SPENCER, BROADCASTER

I have never been to one nor have I had the pleasure to refuse an invitation [to judge a bikini competition]. I would be surprised if they were anything but demeaning and I reckon I've got better things to waste my time on.

DON BRADMAN, CRICKETER

In discussion with his son before he died, said he did not want: *a service for middle-aged male cricket administrators . . . [but instead wanted] . . . young people and women strongly represented.*

2002

EIGHTY-THREE MALE WORKERS AT THE CARTER HOLT HARVEY FACTORY

Refused to accept a pay rise and went on strike until the female office workers at the factory got better pay and conditions too.

2003

MARK HOLDEN, BUSINESS CONSULTANT

[Companies that fail] are usually very blokey old school tie, old boys' networks with few women ... Unless companies get serious about breaking the glass ceiling, they will lose their competitive edge to the enlightened ones.

2004

ADAM GOODES, AFL PLAYER

Said his mum was his inspiration and took her to the Brownlow dinner.

WIL ANDERSON, COMEDIAN

The hard drinking, hard playing and perpetual hard ons of rugby league who have proved they are the kind of scrum sucking pigs only professional sport can throw up.

WILLIAM PETLEY, *SUN HERALD*

Germaine Greer . . . stood out in a room full of women who have 'enjoyed' many a procedure with her no-nonsense, striking presence.

GUILLAUME BRAHIMI, CELEBRITY CHEF

On the fact that eight of the fifteen chefs at the Guillaume at Bennelong restaurant are women:

There isn't so much testosterone in the kitchen. They tend to show greater dedication to the industry from a younger age.

JUSTICE MICHAEL KIRBY, HIGH COURT OF AUSTRALIA

[Justice Meagher's] dismissiveness of women is a relic of an old culture learned in boys-only schools that dominated the legal profession for centuries and captured R.P. Meagher when a youth.

PETER SENIOR, GOLFER

I don't give a rat's a . . . whether she plays or not . . . It's good hype and Laura [Davies] is no mug golfer. I wouldn't mind being picked to play with her.

THE CONSTRUCTION FORESTRY MINING AND ENERGY UNION

We've also succeeded in getting women's toilets, so the ladies are relieved.

MICHAEL MONAGHAN,
MANLY SEA EAGLES RUGBY LEAGUE CAPTAIN

Supported the campaign of Football Fans Against Sexual Assault, saying:
Sexual assault is a cowardly act.

2005

KEYSAR TRAD, LEBANESE MOSLEM ASSOCIATION

We read with dismay comments . . . by an Australian Muslim about women's dress. Islam teaches its followers self-control and to refrain from making judgment on either the basis of their dress or appearance.

LACHLAN MURDOCH, NEWS LIMITED

Came back to live in Australia because his wife asked him to.

2006

GOUGH WHITLAM, FORMER PRIME MINISTER

One of the great things about the federal parliament now is that I think there is about a third of them women. You saw the benefit of that in the vote on the RU486.

JOHN SINGLETON, ADVERTISING GURU

On soccer players faking injuries:
You wouldn't see a netball team go down like that.

PAUL 'FATTY' VAUTIN, *THE FOOTY SHOW*

I support women playing rugby league.

GEORGE BROWNING,
ANGLICAN BISHOP OF CANBERRA AND GOULBURN

Said to his diocese:

I would hope that when I retire you will feel able to nominate a woman.

JUSTICE MICHAEL MCHUGH,
HIGH COURT OF AUSTRALIA

There are at least ten women judges serving on supreme courts of the states and the Federal Court who would make first class High Court judges. I think there is an overpowering case to appoint a woman as my successor.

2007

IAN HEALY, FORMER AUSTRALIAN WICKET KEEPER

On the Barker Old Boy who attacked the selection of
Alyssa Healy in the school First XI:

Did he name any of these wonderful athletes Barker has put out [by selecting Alyssa]? I wouldn't waste my breath on this guy.

KEVIN RUDD, FEDERAL OPPOSITION LEADER

This is the age of professional women who run their own companies, who have their own lives and are not simply the appendages of middle-aged men.

ANDREW O'KEEFE, GAME SHOW HOST

Domestic violence is a misleading term, because it leads you to believe it's a private issue. It's not. It's a public issue, and it's a crime.

RUSSELL CROWE,
ACTOR AND SOUTH SYDNEY RABBITOHS CO-OWNER

Cheerleaders make women uncomfortable and blokes who take their kids to the football also uncomfortable. We felt we didn't need cheerleaders and would like them replaced by a group of drummers, male and female.

the elaines
remarks by women least helpful
to the sisterhood

Unlike the Good Ernie there has never been any debate about what to call the trophy for Remarks Least Helpful to the Sisterhood. The Elaine is named after Elaine Nile, Christian Democrat MP and wife of the Reverend Fred Nile, the other Christian Democrat MP in the New South Wales Parliament. On the

occasion of the very first Ernies in 1993 Elaine was making a speech, only metres away, in the Legislative Council attacking the Ernies women for our behaviour.

Elaine has always remained interested in the Ernies story. Just after the 1994 celebration she told the House that she was very honoured to have the award named after her and recounted the time she met us in the lift: 'I know you belong to the sisterhood, but I belong to the motherhood.'[1]

The Elaine, the trophy for which is a female body-builder in a bikini, is often the most hotly contested award. It inspires real bile and offence among the Ernies women, so much so that in 1998 the Elaine's head was mysteriously pulled off.

---

1   She then proceeded to speak to the Chamber about a mother hen being burnt to death while protecting her chicks. We were a little concerned about this allusion.

There were definite crowd favourites over the years: Bettina Arndt, Miranda Devine, Janet Albrechtsen and, quite surprisingly, Pru Goward. After her 1997 nomination, Pru wrote to Ernies stalwart, Margaret Jones, claiming the nomination could 'clearly only have been seen as unfunny denigration'. We never set out to deliberately nominate Pru Goward. She just seemed accident prone.

Some men have tried to get their own back by nominating women for the Elaine. The most notable was Sydney Lord Mayor Frank Sartor, who put up fellow councillor Kathryn Greiner in 1997. But we had the last laugh when Frank, himself, was later nominated.

Elaine highlights have included a spectacularly rowdy boo-off in 1997 between Janette Howard, Janet McDonald and Pauline Hanson. This was only to be rivalled in 1999 by an equally raucous boo-off between Jocelyn Newman and Babette Frances.

We must also admit that the Ernies themselves have been nominated from time to time for mistakes on our part. Jeannette McHugh dobbed us in for the 'fat lady sings' invitation. However, it didn't make the cut. And occasionally great nominations have been ruled out because they weren't particularly sexist like this one, by actor Kate Fitzpatrick about Germaine Greer. 'At one moment she kissed one of them very near its bum, and I remember thinking no woman who kisses a cat there is going to kiss my baby'. The Elaine has rigorous standards.

1994

WENDY JONES, NSW LIBERAL CANDIDATE

Believed her recently widowed Labor opponent should
not stand for election, saying:

*I have some concerns that perhaps now is not the best time for Gabrielle to be
standing. I guess the majority of mothers out there would share that view.
From a mother's point of view I'd be focused on my child.*

1995

BLANCHE D'ALPUGET,
AUTHOR AND BOB HAWKE'S NEW BRIDE

I do.

DAME LEONIE KRAMER,
SYDNEY UNIVERSITY CHANCELLOR

On why women academics don't get promoted:

They go limp when things get tough.

KATE FISCHER, MODEL

I'm beautiful, I'm a model, I'm allowed to be dumb.

1996

KATHRYN GREINER, CITY OF SYDNEY COUNCILLOR

*I do criticise women . . . who like to be treated as equals and yet, when the
time comes, they suddenly find that something impinges upon
them in terms of their family commitments.*

JOCELYN NEWMAN, FEDERAL MINISTER FOR WOMEN

Said she could not recall reading any feminist books:
I don't think [I got] very much from feminist literature, to be honest.

1997

JANET MCDONALD, JANETTE HOWARD'S FRIEND

*I worry about workplace childcare. I don't want my
cleaner to bring her daughter to the job.*

PAULINE HANSON, FEDERAL ONE NATION MP

*I think the most downtrodden person in this country is the white Anglo-Saxon male. It's
got to the stage where the balance has swung too far and men don't know what to do.*

JANETTE HOWARD, WIFE OF THE PRIME MINISTER

Called Hilary Rodham Clinton 'Mrs Bill Clinton' during her visit to Australia.

JACKIE KELLY, FEDERAL LIBERAL MP

On Amanda Vanstone:

She's fat. You have a problem with that? . . . I didn't comment on her dress sense.

1998

BETTINA ARNDT, FAIRFAX COLUMNIST

*If we are angry about men because they haven't changed enough,
we have to understand where they are coming from … Have we really
tried enough to see the issues from the male perspective?*

KIRSTEN BURGOYNE, DESIRE BRAND MANAGEMENT

Nobody wants to buy lipstick being modelled on a big, fat, frumpy woman.

DR HELEN HUGHES, AUSTRALIAN NATIONAL UNIVERSITY

In a pay equity case:
Hairdressing is not a real trade.

BETTINA ARNDT, FAIRFAX COLUMNIST

*Employers are aware of the precipitous drop in productivity
and soaring phone bills during those after-school hours when working
mothers try to make that connection.*

KATE FISCHER, ACTOR

I am an actress, not an actor. If you call me an actor, people will think I am a lesbian.

HEATHER HILL,

QUEENSLAND ONE NATION SENATE CANDIDATE

On One Nation's policy to replace the Family Court with a 'People's Tribunal':

Men are now disadvantaged, not women . . . Children of broken homes
have to realise that a child's standard of living following divorce cannot
be maintained at a pre-divorce level.

PAULINE HANSON, FEDERAL ONE NATION MP

Single mothers should not get payments after their first child.

1999

JOCELYN NEWMAN, FEDERAL MINISTER FOR WOMEN

On the high cost of childcare for low income earners:

If they can't afford it they have other options.

BABETTE FRANCIS, WOMEN WHO WANT TO BE WOMEN

The feminist movement by flaunting the right to promiscuity and megaphoning
'I'm on the Pill, I'm safe and available,' has cheapened us all, and it is not
surprising if undisciplined men 'try their luck' in the workplace and
regard any initial rejection as 'coyness.'

PROFESSOR JOAN RYDON, SYDNEY UNIVERSITY

Criticised the academic discipline of women's studies, saying:
It has been founded upon some notion that women have been exploited or
frustrated in a world dominated by men . . . rather than to emphasise
a disinterested pursuit of knowledge.

2000

MIRANDA DEVINE, NEWS LIMITED COLUMNIST

Instead of pillorying skinny models and actresses we should be thanking them for
performing a valuable public service. They are the inspiration for young women
to be thin. They help maintain the social stigma that controls obesity.
The odd anorexic is a small price to pay.

MRS ELAINE NILE, NSW CHRISTIAN DEMOCRATS MP

I don't know how much I earn—I just give it to Fred and he puts it in an account.

2001

PRU GOWARD,
FEDERAL SEX DISCRIMINATION COMMISSIONER

Feminists have failed the women on low incomes.
Don't even get me started on it. It really pisses me off.

PAULINE HANSON, ONE NATION LEADER

Putting dinner on the table is more my job than a man's. I'm not a feminist.
I like fussing around the home, clothes washed and ironed and a hot
meal on the table. I like to cook . . . roasts, stew, cheesecake,
lemon meringue pie, fruitcake and biscuits . . .

2002

BETTINA ARNDT, FAIRFAX COLUMNIST

On the fact that Victorian MP Anna Burke did not reveal she
was pregnant during an election campaign:

Burke didn't give voters that option . . . [She] hid the fact that she was pregnant
. . . 'No male in parliament has ever been questioned about his ability to be a
father and an MP at the same time,' was her glib comment.

JANET ALBRECHTSEN, NEWS LIMITED COLUMNIST

If men are commitment-phobic, 1960s feminism made them so.

AMANDA VANSTONE,
FEDERAL MINISTER FOR COMMUNITY SERVICES

During the GST debate said feminine hygiene products were:
trivialities for most women.

2003

SALLY LOANE, BROADCASTER

*The Teachers' Federation says that . . . teachers are getting 24 per cent less than
the average male weekly earnings. Which begs the question really, because
the majority of teachers are . . . females, so maybe that figure of male average
weekly earnings isn't quite as relevant.*

BETTINA ARNDT, FAIRFAX COLUMNIST

*The married man today rarely has rights to control his own leisure.
Hell, no. He's now on a leash, a very short leash.*

MIRANDA DEVINE, NEWS LIMITED COLUMNIST

After once writing that a few anorexics is a small price to pay for defeating obesity I was branded anti-woman and given an 'Elaine' sexism award ... But we should be encouraging skinny role models. After all, vanity is the most powerful tool we have for controlling obesity.

MARGARET COURT, TENNIS GREAT

Agreed with Damir Dokic about the number of lesbians in women's tennis: *A few of the older ones were 'that way'. Younger players were sort of snared in with 'it' and then we finished up having quite a lot of 'them' on tour that were like 'that'.*

SANDRA KANCK, SA DEMOCRAT MP

Named the factions in the Australian Democrats—one led by Natasha Stott Despoja and one by Meg Lees as: *The Pert Breast Faction and the Breasts Less Pert Faction.*

JANET ALBRECHTSEN, NEWS LIMITED COLUMNIST

Why did the feminists have to go and ruin everything?

2004

JACKIE KELLY, FEDERAL LIBERAL MP

No one in my electorate is interested in a university education. Penrith is pram city.

NORMA PLUMMER, AUSTRALIAN NETBALL COACH

Called the World Champion Kiwi team:
a bunch of scrubbers.

HELEN MCCABE, NEWS LIMITED COLUMNIST

*In nightclubs across the world there are sexual predators. Not men, but women
. . . When talking to the young men who play elite sport, it is clear they are privy
to a world where women offer or demand a full range of sexual favours.*

JULIE FITZGERALD, SYDNEY SWIFTS NETBALL COACH

On Netball Australia's new President, Marylin Melhuish:
*She is not like one of those old bags who's been around
netball for years, she'll be sensational.*

BETTINA ARNDT, FAIRFAX COLUMNIST

Men are always at risk of the supposed 'accident', when the woman may decide she is ready even if the man is not.

JANET ALBRECHTSEN, NEWS LIMITED COLUMNIST

*Affirmative action does no one any favours.
Who wants to score a job on sex, not merit?*

2005

COLLEEN MCCULLOUGH, AUTHOR

Said the Pitcairn men convicted of raping young girls were just following their 'custom':

It's Polynesian to break your girls in at twelve.

LOUISE MARKUS, FEDERAL LIBERAL MP

Men were often the victims of their own crimes, because they felt bad after committing violence on their female partners.

2006

DANNA VALE, FEDERAL LIBERAL MP

*We are at risk of being overwhelmed by Muslims bearing large families
while we are aborting ourselves almost out of existence.*

CLOVER MOORE, CITY OF SYDNEY LORD MAYOR

On her new deputy:

*There'll be a lot of things for Verity to do. She'll have
to get herself a hat and a pair of gloves.*

KATHRYN GREINER, LIBERAL PARTY IDENTITY

On Federal Minister Helen Coonan:

She didn't need to join the hairy armpit brigade.

2007

ALISON VENESS-MCGOURTY,
HARPER'S BAZAAR EDITOR

*She [Princess Mary] is fast becoming a fashion frump. It might be because
of her pregnancy but that isn't really an excuse these days.*

JANET ALBRECHTSEN, NEWS LIMITED COLUMNIST

Referred to:

... the banalities bandied about by Australian feminists obsessed with glass ceilings, pay discrepancies and men not changing the right number of nappies.

BETTINA ARNDT, *SUNDAY TASMANIAN*

So what if the average woman in Australian earns $300 less per week than the average man?

THE ERNIES DISHONOUR BOARD

	Gold	Silver – Industrial	Silver – Political
1993	Joe de Bruyn		
1994	Terry Griffiths MP	Lance Jamieson	Terry Griffiths MP
1995	Justice John Gallop	Martin Ferguson	Michael Hodgman MP
1996	Magistrate Ron Gething	The Law Society of NSW	Bob Katter MP
1997	Michael Knight MP	Telstra	Michael Knight MP
1998	Judge Nigel Clarke	HPM Industries	Tony Smith & Iain Maclean
1999	Magistrate #1	Steggles	Michael Thompson & Queensland Young Liberals
2000	Nick Bideau	Michael Costa	Michael Woolridge
2001	John Howard PM	John Elliott & Mark Mentha	Ron Best MP & John Howard PM
2002	Archbishop Pell	Dick Warburton	Tony Abbott MP
2003	Stellar Call Centre	Stellar Call Centre	Brendan Smyth MP
2004	Tooheys	Australia Post	John Howard PM
2005	Sheik Feiz Mohammad	Tara Anglican Girls School	Brendan Nelson MP
2006	P & O Cruises	P & O Cruises	Senator Bill Heffernan

THE ERNIES DISHONOUR BOARD

	Silver – Media	Silver – Judicial	The Warney for Sport
1993			
1994	Peter Smark & Bernard Zuel	Justices Bland & Bollen	
1995	P.P. McGuinness	Justice John Gallop	
1996	Jeff Wells	Magistrate Ron Gething	
1997	John Laws & David Barnett	Judge Nigel Clarke	
1998	Robert Manne	Judge Nigel Clarke	
1999	P.P. McGuinness	Magistrate #1	
2000	D.D. McNicholl	Justice Kennedy	Nick Bideau
2001	Mark Patrick	Magistrate Steven Scarlett	Cameron Williams
2002	Andrew Bolt	High Court of Australia	Ray Hadley
2003	Ron Casey	Justice Roddy Meagher	Damir Dokic
2004	P.P. McGuinness	Barrister Paul Reynolds	Malcolm Noad
2005	Dave Richardson	Barrister John Dorris & Ian Harrison QC	Willie Mason
2006	Jeff Corbett	Chris Papadopoulos	Grant Birse

THE ERNIES DISHONOUR BOARD

The Fred – Clerical, Culinary, Celebrity	The Clinton – For repeat offenders	The Elaine – For women	The Good Ernie
		Wendy Jones	Peter Sams
		Blanche D'Alpuget	Australian Manufacturing Workers Union
		Clr Kathryn Greiner	Ernie Page MP
		Janet McDonald	Peter Cameron
	John Howard PM	Bettina Arndt	Ernie Page MP
	Piers Akerman & Alan Jones	Senator Jocelyn Newman	George Trumbull
	John Howard PM	Miranda Devine	Bob Carr MP
Archbishop Jensen	John Howard PM	Pru Goward	Bob Debus, Matt Foley, Rob Hulls & Peter Patmore
Archbishop Pell	Tony Abbott MP	Bettina Arndt	Carter Holt Harvey Workers
Neil Perry	John Howard PM	Sally Loane	Mark Holden
Tooheys	Tony Abbott MP	Jackie Kelly MP	Adam Goodes
Sheik Feiz Mohammad	Tony Abbott MP	Colleen McCullough	Keysar Trad
Tom Cruise & Peter West	Tony Abbott MP	Danna Vale MP	Rt Hon. Gough Whitlam

index

photo credits

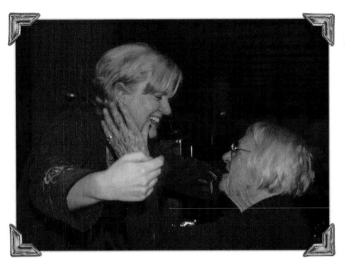